THE NEW
Health Care
System

THE NEW
Health Care System

Everything You Need to Know

David Nather

THOMAS DUNNE BOOKS
St. Martin's Griffin
New York

BP45

THOMAS DUNNE BOOKS.
An imprint of St. Martin's Press.

www.thomasdunnebooks.com
www.stmartins.com

ISBN 978-0-312-64934-0

First Edition: July 2010

10 9 8 7 6 5 4 3 2 1

12/1/10

To Elissa, Jessa, and Gabe

Contents

Introduction   1

1   How Health Insurance Works   6

2   Fixing the Insurance Market   25

3   Everyone Has to Have Health Coverage   37

4   Getting Help Paying for Coverage   48

5   What Employers Have to Do   61

6   The New Health Insurance Exchanges   71

7   What's Left of the Public Option?   87

8   While You're Waiting . . .   95

9   Medicare Changes   108

10 The Expansion of Medicaid   119

11 Long-Term Care   130

12 Preventive Care and Wellness   141

13 Who Decides What Care You Get?   149

14 How They'll Cut Costs   158

15 How They'll Pay for It   172

Appendix   195

Acknowledgments   219

Index   223

THE NEW
Health Care
System

Introduction

When President Obama signed health care reform into law on March 23, 2010, a lot of people celebrated. Others worried that civilization was coming to an end. There were victory speeches and high-fives, the occasional brick thrown through a congressional office window, and even death threats against Democrats in Congress. Most people, however, just scratched their heads and tried to figure out what was actually going to happen next.

If you're one of those head-scratchers, this book is for you.

Everyone is going to be trying to figure out what's in it for them, if the new health care system affects them at all. Will your health coverage change if you're at a large, stable company? If you own a small business, will you have to provide health coverage you can't afford? Why is the government going to make everyone get health coverage? Will your premiums go up even faster? Is Grandma about to lose her Medicare benefits? And what on earth is a "health insurance exchange," anyway?

Let's take a quick crack at those questions. If you're at a large company, your health care probably won't change at all, except that you'll get some new protections to help you with big medical bills and keep you from being denied coverage for preexisting conditions. Your small business won't be forced to provide health coverage, but it might be able to get a tax credit to help pay for it—and the new health insurance exchanges should make it easier to get stable coverage. If you don't have coverage at all, you will have to get it—not because President Obama and Congress just like to make you do things, but because those new protections against health insurance loopholes (such as preexisting conditions, lifetime limits, and cancelling coverage for sick people) wouldn't work otherwise. And many of you will be able to get tax credits and subsidies to help pay for it.

Most of you won't see your premiums go up any faster. If you get health insurance on your own, it might get more expensive—because it will cover more things—but more than half of all people will get the subsidies, and those should cancel out the price increase. Despite what you may have heard, Grandma is not about to lose her Medicare benefits, though her health care providers might complain about not being paid enough. And if you want to get a sneak preview of a "health insurance exchange"—the new Web-based marketplaces for small business and individual health insurance, starting in 2014—take a look at the Massachusetts Health Connector (www.mahealthconnector.org), which is an early version of the same thing.

The goal of this book is to help you answer all of those questions and more, and to help you understand why Congress did what it did. First we'll explore how health insurance works, to give you the background you need to understand the rest of this book. Then we'll walk through the big changes the new law makes to the rules of health insurance to try to solve the many problems people have had. You'll learn about the new protections you'll get, and the trade-off—the new rule that everyone has to get health coverage. Without that rule, the new protections would make everyone's health insurance way too expensive.

And you'll learn when everything will happen, what you'll get right away (Chapter 8: "While You're Waiting . . ."), and which changes won't happen until 2014. You'll also learn what new benefits you'll get under Medicare and what's really behind those "cuts" you may have heard about. You'll be able to read about the expansion of Medicaid, to help low-income people get health coverage, and about some important new long-term care programs that you might not have heard about amid all the noise. You'll also get an early look at some of the experiments you might see in the coming years, such as "medical homes" and "accountable care organizations," which will try to cut back on all the money we waste on unnecessary medical care.

Finally, you'll learn how you might be affected by the different ways Congress is going to pay for the new coverage. Yes, you read that right: Congress is actually trying to pay for it. There's a lot of debate about whether they'll really go through with the various taxes and payment cutbacks to health care providers. Congress has a history of reversing itself under pressure. But if they let everything stand, there's a very good chance that health care reform will, in fact, pay for itself.

At the time that health care reform became law, there was so much misunderstanding and bad information in circulation, it's no wonder the country was so divided over it. In a March 2010 tracking poll by the Henry J. Kaiser Family Foundation, for example, four out of ten Americans thought they would have to change the health care they already had. In reality, most of you won't have to change anything. And more than half of all Americans thought the new health care law would increase the deficit, which isn't true. Only 15 percent knew the truth: The Congressional Budget Office, the official budget scorekeeper of Congress, says the new health care law should actually reduce the deficit.

When there's so much confusion about the basics of the new law, the details that most affect our lives are in danger of becoming lost. This book should help you keep track of all the pieces and understand how the new system is supposed to work. It's written in a way that lets you skip around to read about your own situation. If you work for a small business, or have individual insurance, or if you have no health insurance, or you're an early retiree, you can skip to the "What to Do" sections at the end of several of the chapters. If you're on Medicare, you can read the Medicare chapter (Chapter 9) and skip everything else. There's some repetition, and that's deliberate, so you can jump around to different sections without missing important points.

Don't expect this book to cover every possible situation. It can't, because everyone's situation is different. But it will provide enough information to get you started. And to answer the rest of your questions, you'll find a lot of information resources scattered throughout the book—agencies, outside health care groups, Web sites, and phone numbers—that can help you do more research to address your own health care needs.

A lot of you may not notice anything different in the coming years, because most of the law is aimed at the least stable parts of the health care marketplace: health insurance for individuals and small businesses. These groups have the hardest time finding health coverage options that are easy to compare, and the least protection against loopholes that can bankrupt them—or premiums that can shoot through the roof when someone gets sick. Because they have the biggest problems, many of the changes are designed to make life easier for them.

But the law is not just about protecting other people. If you thought you were safe because you had health coverage through the workplace, think again. Under the old health care system, if you lost your job, your stable health coverage would be gone, too. Or your employer could drop your coverage, or scale it way back because it was getting too expensive. If you or a family member had a preexisting condition, under the old system, that would have been it for your or your loved one's health care. Or you'd have found out about the fine print in your coverage too late, when you had a big medical bill that wasn't covered. And none of us was safe from rising health care premiums. The jury is out on whether the new system will get these under control, but we know what the old system was doing about them: nothing.

So what's the bottom line on the new health care system? It won't be socialism. If you'd like someone to tell you that it's socialism, you need a different book. On the other hand, it certainly won't solve all problems. Health insurance won't become dirt cheap, your days of fighting with health care bureaucrats aren't over, and it won't suddenly become easier to find decent health care at nights or on weekends. And health insurance companies will never stop looking for loopholes.

The new law might even run into its own set of problems. This book describes how the system will work if everything described in the law happens the way it's supposed to. But things can go wrong along the way. At this writing, the Department of Health and Human Services is scrambling to decide a lot of the day-to-day details that weren't decided in the law, and it might not have the time or the resources to make all of its deadlines. Too many people might choose to pay the fine rather than get health coverage. The experiments on new ways to slow health care spending might not work well. If they don't, the question many Republicans have been asking—is this new system sustainable?—will come back with a new intensity.

Still, we know we couldn't continue with the old system. It didn't have a future. You might get headaches trying to figure out how all of this is going to work, or wonder how to settle any problems that come up. But you won't be pining for the days when you could be rejected for health coverage just when you needed it the most, or when one illness could throw you into debt for the rest of your life. And you certainly won't wish we could keep wasting money so your premiums could go up even faster.

The health care system is moving on. Now is the time to learn how to make it work for you.

1

How Health Insurance Works

Someone has to pay for the health care we all receive. But health care is expensive, and it's getting more expensive all the time. Some of the increase in costs is for good reasons, such as the new and better medical technologies, procedures, and drugs that are coming out all the time. And some of it is for lousy reasons, such as the doctors who give us more tests and procedures than we really need, and the fact that we tend to pay doctors by how many services they perform rather than how effectively they treat us. For all of these reasons, health care would bankrupt all but the richest of us if we didn't have help paying for it.

Health insurance is the way we spread the cost of everyone's health care and help each other pay for it. It's not supposed to give us free health care. Most of us pay premiums for our coverage—though they're kept low in public programs for low-income people—in order to maintain a pool of money. But insurance is supposed to shield us from the highest costs of health care when we're sick or injured. Some of us will always pay more into our health coverage than we get back, if we're lucky and don't use the health care system much. Some of us get back more than we pay in. But that's the way the social contract of health insurance works: We pay to help ourselves and other people, and when we need help, others help to pay for us.

There are many different forms of health coverage. Most of us get private health insurance through the workplace, and usually our employer shares the costs with us. (Some of them are more generous than others.) And some of us take our chances getting private insurance policies for ourselves, if our workplace doesn't provide it or if we don't have a workplace to get it through. But many of us get it through public programs. If we're sixty-five or older, we get it through Medicare, that government-run health care program for most elderly people and younger people with disabilities. If we're poor or close to the poverty line, and we fall into certain categories, we might get health coverage through Medicaid—which is run by the federal government and the states—and our kids might be covered through the State Children's Health Insurance Program. If we're serving in the military, we get it through TRICARE, and after our service is over, we'll get it through the Veterans Administration.

It's a fragmented system, with different rules for the public programs and 1,300 private health insurance plans. But it evolved that way because those were the collective choices we have made as a country. We have accepted a unified system of coverage for one group—the elderly—under the Medicare program, but generally resisted it otherwise. Most of us have had private health insurance through the workplace since World War II, and most Americans have grown used to that system and want to keep it. For that matter, most Americans prefer private health insurance in general. That's why, except for vulnerable groups such as the elderly and the poor, our political system has resisted any big expansion of the role of government in health care.

But there are certain things that all forms of health coverage have in common. To work well, they have to spread the costs of the healthy and the sick so that it all more or less averages out. If any health insurance plan can't do that, it risks losing all the healthy people and keeping only the ones who have lots of health problems. In the health care industry, this is called "adverse selection." It's not a problem for programs with large pools of people, such as Medicare, because they have enough participants to spread the costs fairly easily. And it's not a big problem for any private insurance plan with lots of people in it, such as a large company's health care plan. But the smaller the pool, the bigger the problem becomes. That's one reason why small businesses have so much trouble finding affordable coverage for their workers. And that's why anyone in an individual or family health insurance plan is the most vulnerable of all—because there is no one else to share the risks with you.

"Death Spirals" and Preexisting Conditions

If a health insurance plan gets stuck with mostly people who need a lot of health care, and few healthy people to help share those costs, it has to bring more money in to cover the expenses. That means raising the premiums. So suddenly everyone in the plan is paying more every month just to keep their insurance. The healthy people might decide to leave and find another plan that won't charge them so much, or they might just go without coverage. If this continues long enough, it creates what's called a "death spiral," where the pool of people gets smaller and smaller until only the people with the costliest health conditions are left. This is why private health insurance companies go to such lengths to keep their pool of people, on average, as close to the general health of the population as possible.

Other countries that also have competing health insurance plans face the same dilemma. They, too, have to find ways to keep enough money coming in to cover all of their costs. But in the United States, we have another factor on top of that: the profit motive. Ours is the only industrialized country that bases so much of its health care system on private health insurance companies that have to answer to their shareholders. Even in Germany, where the health plans are called "sickness funds" and compete for customers much like ours do, the health plans aren't allowed to make profits. Instead, they compete in other ways, such as offering extra benefits or paying claims faster than the other plans.

All of this helps explain why health insurance companies in this country have used tactics that have made them so unpopular. They have tried to avoid paying for the people who need health care the most. They have refused to cover people with "preexisting conditions," or refused to cover the conditions themselves, or made people go through a waiting period before the conditions would be covered. In some of the most notorious cases, they have used a practice called "rescissions": cancelling people's coverage retroactively if they found a crucial, and sometimes not so crucial, piece of information that the patient didn't disclose when he applied for coverage.

These are the kinds of extremes that insurance companies have gone to in order to avoid attracting too many expensive patients, and that's what the new health care reform law is supposed to prevent from happening. But the pressures will always be there for insurance companies to cover their costs and keep them as stable as possible. If they can't keep you out of their plan for having a health condition, and they can't hike your individual premiums through the roof so you'll take the hint and leave their pool—two practices that would be banned under the new law—they can just make everyone's premiums more expensive. But now that everyone will be required to have health insurance, and insurers can get lots of young and healthy new customers, they may not feel the need to raise premiums for everyone to cover the most expensive customers. But if lots of healthy people avoid the new requirement, the insurance companies could charge everyone higher premiums and say they had no choice.

Different Kinds of Private Health Plans

- **Health Maintenance Organization (HMO):** A health care system that provides health care through a tight network of doctors and hospitals and assumes the financial risk for the services. You're likely to face the most restrictions in this model, since you have to stay within the network, but you probably will pay less for the coverage.

- **Preferred Provider Organization (PPO):** A health plan that uses looser networks of doctors and hospitals. You'll probably have a greater selection with this kind of plan, but you'll have to pay more for it. You can also go outside the network and pay a greater share of charges for services.

- **Point of Service (POS):** A hybrid between an HMO and a PPO, in that it acts more like an HMO within the network of doctors and hospitals and like a PPO outside the network.

- **Fee for Service (FFS):** The oldest kind of health insurance plan, in which the patient chooses any doctor or hospital and the insurance simply pays for the services rendered. This kind of insurance fell out of favor when businesses began to turn to managed care plans, which monitor costs more closely before deciding whether to cover them.

- **Health Savings Account (HSA):** A special account that allows people to save money on a pre-tax or tax-deductible basis and use it to pay for their health care expenses up to a certain level. An HSA is used together with high-deductible health plans, which have lower premiums than other plans but don't cover your health costs until you've spent a fairly large amount of money on your own. As of 2010, these plans had to have deductibles of at least $1,200 for individual coverage and $2,400 for family coverage.

How to Look for Insurance

Even under the new system, you'll encounter some basic trade-offs when shopping for private health insurance. Here's the biggest one: The more you want to avoid paying for medical expenses out of pocket, the higher your premiums will be. When choosing a plan, one of your most important decisions will be how often you think you'll need to see a doctor, and how much of a risk you want to take on high out-of-pocket expenses in order to keep your monthly premiums low.

With any health insurance plan, you pay in several different ways. You pay your monthly premium to maintain the coverage, but you'll also pay something on your own to share the expenses of the medical care. Depending on the plan, you might pay any or all of the following: copayments for visits to the doctor or hospital, copayments for prescription drugs, coinsurance (where you pay a certain percentage of the bill), or a deductible (where your coverage kicks in only after you've paid a certain amount out of pocket).

If you're looking at a selection of health plans, and you're tempted to pick the one with the cheapest monthly premium, take a closer look. There's probably a reason why it's so cheap. Most likely the copayments, coinsurance, or deductibles—and maybe all three—will be higher than under a more generous plan with a higher premium. That might be the right risk for you to take. If you don't expect you or your family to have many health care needs, it may not make much sense to pay a lot in premiums each month. But if you do run into an unexpected medical emergency, you might be exposed to more costs than you would have been under a plan with higher premiums.

This is an especially big problem for people buying health insurance on their own rather than getting it through the workplace. If you get health coverage at work, you probably won't have a wide range of choices—an HMO and a PPO from the same insurance company might be your only options. But they probably will protect you fairly well, if you work for a medium-size or large company that treats its employees well. If you work for a small business or a retail chain that doesn't provide a lot of benefits, or if you've just lost a job and need to get coverage on your own, you need to be on the lookout for bad deals.

One of the biggest problems has been the rise of "limited benefit" health plans, which are advertised as a way for people to get at least some coverage at an affordable price. They're offered to people buying health insurance on their own, but they're especially popular among businesses with hourly workers who wouldn't be able to offer them any coverage otherwise. The catch, of course, is that "limited benefit" means exactly what it says. The plans might have extremely tight limits on how much they'll pay in a given year, or low limits on how much they'll pay for each day in a hospital. So if you go over that limit—which is likely with any kind of serious medical problem—you'll be stuck with the remaining bills.

Limited benefit plans have had strong political appeal in recent years, especially in Florida, where the state created the Cover Florida Health Care Access Program in 2008 to offer cheap coverage to uninsured people. But look closely at the plans, and you'll understand why they're so cheap. One carrier, for example, offers two plans with no prescription drug coverage, and two that cover drugs but only pay up to $1,000 a year for them. One plan covers only $40,000 a year in total medical benefits. The carrier's "preventive" plans don't cover hospital inpatient services at all, while its "catastrophic" plans charge $500 in copayments for the first five days. And if you needed emergency care at a hospital in your network, you could expect to pay a $250 copayment for it. Those are much higher copayments, and much lower coverage limits, than you'd find in a typical comprehensive health care plan, the kind offered by most reputable companies.

The new health care law is supposed to crack down on these kinds of skimpy benefits by defining a new minimum of what health plans for individuals and small businesses should cover. Those requirements would apply only to plans offered after 2014 by the new health insurance exchanges, which will be Web-based marketplaces where you can go in every state for one-stop shopping for health insurance. But the hope is that most insurance companies will phase out the limited benefit plans so all of their products will be in line with what's offered in the exchanges. This could take a while, though. So for the time being, it's a good idea to keep your eyes open so you don't get stuck with a lot less protection than you thought you had.

In 2009, Consumers Union came out with a handy list of seven clues that a health plan might be "junk"—not enough protection for the money you're paying in premiums. The new law should stop most of these practices eventually, but the biggest changes don't kick in for a few years. So until that happens, it's worth keeping the following tips in mind as you look over your options:

1. Never buy coverage that calls itself a "limited benefit" plan or "not major medical" insurance.
2. Watch out for anything that has low limits on the total benefits it will pay out. Even $100,000 won't protect you from a big financial hit if you or a member of your family has a major illness.
3. Look out for any plan where the premium seems unusually low.

4. Read the plan carefully to make sure all major items are covered, especially basic benefits such as prescription drugs. If you don't see it mentioned, it probably isn't covered.
5. Watch for tight limits on what a plan covers for certain types of care, such as a dollar limit on how much it covers for each day in the hospital.
6. Make sure it mentions an "out-of-pocket maximum"—how much you have to pay yourself before the plan starts covering everything. And watch out for loopholes in the plan, such as not counting copayments toward your out-of-pocket limit.
7. Look closely for any unusual limits, such as not covering hospital care until the second day.

Loopholes

Even when you're comparing comprehensive plans that don't have big gaps in coverage, there can be loopholes that seem minor but will make a big difference if you get seriously ill. The new law should make these less likely, but it's a good idea to know what to look for in the meantime—and to be an informed consumer so you can keep your eyes open even under the new system.

The issue of what counts toward your out-of-pocket limit, for example, is an important one. Some health plans count your deductible and coinsurance payments toward that limit, but not the copayments that you hand over every time you visit a doctor's office or the hospital. In those cases your "out-of-pocket limit" isn't what you think it is. And over time, if you have a major illness or injury, those copayments can add up quickly. So when comparing two plans, if they seem pretty much the same, but one counts copayments toward the out-of-pocket limit and the other doesn't, your best choice is the plan that counts them.

For most people who haven't had a lot of health problems, the hardest thing to do is to anticipate how much protection you would have under any given health plan—and how much you would have to pay on your own—if you were unlucky enough to suffer a serious illness. But that's exactly what you have to think about when buying health insurance. After all, it's not the occasional cold or flu that could bankrupt you. A woman who is diagnosed with breast cancer, for example, faces treatment costs that can easily run into six figures, not counting insurance coverage. A May 2009 study by the Georgetown University Health Policy Institute and the Center for American Progress Action Fund calculated that a breast cancer patient could face eighty-seven weeks of treatment, costing a total of $97,298 in California and $143,180 in Massachusetts—before any insurance was counted—because of the differences in what doctors around the country charge for their services.

So it's important to find a plan that protects you from as many of those expenses as possible. But when the Georgetown researchers studied actual individual health insurance policies in those two states, they found that a breast cancer patient in Massachusetts would pay two wildly different amounts on her own under two plans that were similar in almost every way. The big difference: One plan counted copayments toward the out-of-pocket limit, the other didn't. Under the plan that counted copayments toward the limit, the breast cancer patient would have paid $7,641 over the course of her treatment. That's a lot for anyone to pay, but it's not as much as she would have paid under the plan that didn't count copayments. If she had signed up for that one, she would have paid $12,907 on her own.

The Massachusetts example is an important one, because that state has a system similar to what the new health care law is trying to create throughout the country. In 2006, the state reformed its health care system to set up a "Health Connector," an exchange that offers health insurance to individuals and small businesses in Massachusetts—much like the exchanges the new federal law creates for everyone. It standardizes the kinds of benefits plans offer, so all plans fit into one of four categories: gold, silver, bronze, and "young adult." The gold plans offer the most generous coverage but cost the most each month, while the young adult plans offer the least protection but also cost the least. But even when the differences between the plans are narrowed that much, they still have subtle distinctions that could matter greatly to someone who got seriously ill. That's why it's a good idea to learn as much as you can about the fine print before you sign up.

When the new state-based health insurance exchanges start up in 2014, you'll have access to a lot more information to research your options. For now, though, it isn't always easy to find out ahead of time whether a particular health insurance plan has these kinds of loopholes, even if you know what to look for. The "evidence of coverage" document that comes with an insurance plan is the most comprehensive list of what is and isn't covered, but it's often hard to read—it's usually full of legalese—and most people aren't allowed to see it until they're already enrolled in the plan. Plan brochures are often available online, as are lists of services that aren't covered. These documents can help you check for big-ticket items that you would have to pay for yourself, such as chemotherapy. But otherwise, they may not tell you what you need to know about more subtle gaps. Aetna, for example, is at least honest enough to include a footnote in the brochure for its Aetna Advantage Plans warning that "copay does not count towards coinsurance or out-of-pocket maximum." Other brochures, however, aren't so clear.

If you've just left a job in which you had health coverage, you may also have the option of staying on your employer's health insurance plan. This option is called COBRA Continuation Health Coverage, and it can help you avoid having to look for decent coverage on your own. You usually can get COBRA coverage if your workplace offered health coverage and has twenty or more employees. The catch, however, is that COBRA is incredibly expensive. You have to pay the entire premium yourself, plus a 2 percent administrative fee. That's why so few people have used COBRA coverage in the past.

However, for the next few years, it may still be your best bet as a temporary measure while you apply for cheaper coverage. Until 2014, adults can still be denied coverage for preexisting conditions, so it may be a good idea to keep the COBRA coverage until you have been accepted for individual insurance. There will also be a temporary high-risk pool available for people with preexisting conditions, but those can be expensive, too. So before you drop COBRA, you might want to research the high-risk pool in your state to see if it would really give you cheaper and better coverage. (See Chapter 8 for more on the temporary high-risk pool program.)

Starting in 2014, you'll be able to get individual insurance through the new health insurance exchanges, and they won't be able to turn you down because of preexisting conditions. And if your income is low enough, you may be able to get subsidies to help you pay for the coverage, so this probably will be a cheaper option than COBRA. Even then, though, it may take a while for a health plan to process your paperwork, so it may still make sense to go on COBRA temporarily until you are approved for your new coverage.

What to Do If You Run into Trouble

If you have signed up for health insurance and your insurance company is refusing to pay for something, your first step is to file an appeal directly with the insurance company. They should have instructions on their Web site on how to do this, and they'll probably have appeal forms available. You should file your appeal quickly, because most insurance companies will set a deadline for appealing any of their decisions to deny coverage. If you don't file in time, you may be out of luck. If you need help filing the appeal, some state insurance agencies offer assistance. And if you're getting your coverage through the workplace, your human resources director might be able to help.

A good way to prepare for your appeal is to read the insurer's "evidence of coverage" document for proof that the service should have been covered. (Once you're enrolled, you should be able to get that document directly from the insurance company.) If you find proof that the service is covered, and you can point to the exact section and wording, you have a much better chance of getting the insurance company to pay for it. If you can't find that proof—or, even worse, if you find a loophole that says the service isn't covered—your odds of success are a lot lower. It might also help to get a letter from your doctor explaining why he believes the service is medically necessary, in case the insurance company is trying to argue that it isn't.

If your appeal to the insurance company fails, you can also file a complaint with your state insurance agency, which regulates most private insurance plans. They can't get actively involved on your behalf, but they can investigate and ask your health insurance company to explain their decision—and make sure that they're complying with state laws. In some cases, that may be enough to get your insurance company to take a second look. No insurance company wants to rack up too many complaints. (Some state insurance agencies track complaints and make those lists available to the public.)

In some states, you can also ask for an external review, in which an outside group of medical experts double-checks the decision to make sure the health plan is following its own rules. Under the new federal health care law, you'll be able to get an external review in all states as of September 2010—though only for new health plans, not current ones. For now, according to the Patient Advocate Foundation, a Virginia-based advocacy group, eighteen states give patients the right to ask for an external review: Arizona, California, Connecticut, Florida, Hawaii, Illinois, Maryland, Minnesota, Missouri, New Jersey, New Mexico,

New York, Ohio, Pennsylvania, Rhode Island, Tennessee, Texas, and Vermont. Some health plans also allow you to ask for external reviews, although sometimes they charge a fee for the review.

You can also check with the Department of Labor, which enforces the Employee Retirement Income Security Act (ERISA), a federal law that sets rules for health and disability benefits obtained through the workplace. The department's Employee Benefits Security Administration can tell you what your rights are if your health plan hasn't followed the ERISA rules. If you get your health coverage through a "self-insured" plan—in which your employer assumes all of the financial risk and pays all of the health care claims itself—the Department of Labor may be your only option, since self-insured plans are exempt from state regulation. About a third of all Americans who get their health coverage through the workplace get it through self-insured plans.

Finally, if all else fails and you believe a service should have been covered, you can talk to an attorney about suing the insurance company. But lawsuits are expensive, they take forever to resolve, and you may not prevail. And if it's a self-insured plan, your lawsuit rights under ERISA are limited. You might be able to recover the cost of the benefit, for example, but you won't be able to sue for damages. So it's worth thinking about it seriously before moving ahead, and it's probably worth your while only if a truly life-threatening or expensive medical service is at stake.

Glossary of Insurance Terms

Claim: A request for payment by the doctor or hospital.

Coinsurance: The percentage of the medical expenses you have to cover after you've paid the deductible.

Copayment: A fixed amount you have to pay for an office visit or for a prescription drug before your insurance pays the rest.

Deductible: A fixed amount you have to pay on your own over the course of a year before your insurance starts to cover most of your costs.

Exclusions: Specific services that your insurance won't cover.

External review: An appeal to an outside body of medical experts that looks at your health plan's decision to deny coverage for a service. This is not available everywhere yet, but the new law will make it more widely available starting in September 2010.

Internal review: Your appeal to a health insurance company to review its own decision to deny coverage for a service.

Preexisting condition: A medical condition that you already had when you first signed up for coverage.

Premium: The amount you pay every month to stay insured.

Reinsurance: A kind of protection that some insurance companies use to insure themselves.

Underwriting: The process of reviewing your medical history and status to decide how much to charge you for your coverage. It has also been used in the past to reject people who applied for coverage, or to refuse to cover certain things.

RESOURCES

The **Department of Health and Human Services** is the federal government's main regulator of health care safety net programs throughout the nation. It contains agencies that oversee important programs, including the **Centers for Medicare & Medicaid Services,** which sets rules for the Medicare and Medicaid programs. Other important agencies include the **Administration on Aging,** which focuses on long-term care and other programs for seniors; the **Centers for Disease Control and Prevention,** which is in charge of public health; the **Food and Drug Administration,** which regulates prescription drugs; and the **Indian Health Service,** which provides federal health services to native Americans.

Department of Health and Human Services
200 Independence Avenue, SW
Washington, DC 20201
1-877-696-6775
www.hhs.gov

The **Department of Labor's Employee Benefits Security Administration** enforces the ERISA standards and offers several helpful consumer guides on health insurance, including specific laws and the rules for filing appeals. Your regional office of the administration may also be able to help you if you're having trouble getting your health plan to cover something and your appeal to the plan wasn't successful.

Department of Labor
200 Constitution Avenue, NW
Washington, DC 20210
1-866-487-2365
Department of Labor consumer guides:
www.dol.gov/ebsa/consumer_info_health.html
(To find your nearest regional office of the Employee Benefits Security Administration, call 1-866-444-3272.)

State insurance agencies will be your best source of information on how to search for health coverage, which insurance companies have the best customer satisfaction ratings, and what to do if you have a problem. The **National Association of Insurance Commissioners** has an interactive map on its Web site that can help you find your state's insurance agency.

www.naic.org/state_web_map.htm

The Web site **eHealthInsurance.com,** a private service based in California, has a good search engine to help you compare prices for different health plans in your area. With partnerships with more than 180 health insurance companies, it offers a good selection. It includes private health insurance for individuals and small businesses, Medicare supplemental coverage, Medicare Advantage and prescription drug coverage, and long-term care insurance.

eHealthInsurance
11919 Foundation Place
Gold River, CA 95670
1-800-977-8860
www.ehealthinsurance.com

The consumer group **Families USA** has put together a series of guides to help people find health insurance in every state, and fact sheets about individual insurance and health savings accounts. It also has links to more detailed guides on how health insurance works and how to resolve disputes.

Families USA
1201 New York Avenue, NW, Suite 1100

Washington, DC 20005
(202) 628-3030
www.familiesusa.org

Consumers Union, the publisher of *Consumer Reports*, has a useful section on looking for health insurance, including the seven signs that a health plan might be "junk" insurance. It also has occasional articles on insurance, hospitals, and nursing homes, and other ratings, and it recommends the best and most cost-effective drugs for certain conditions.

Consumers Union
101 Truman Avenue
Yonkers, NY 10703-1057
(914) 378-2000
www.consumerreports.org/health

The **Patient Advocate Foundation** helps mediate disputes between patients and their insurers over coverage for serious illnesses, and helps the patients sort out job and medical debt problems. It also has produced several useful consumer publications, including a "managed care answer guide," which includes advice on how to choose an insurance plan, and a guide to the appeals process.

Patient Advocate Foundation
700 Thimble Shoals Blvd., Suite 200
Newport News, VA 23606
1-800-532-5274
www.patientadvocate.org

The **Georgetown University Health Policy Institute** has created a Web site called Healthinsuranceinfo.net, which supplies "Consumer Guides for Getting and Keeping Health Insurance" for all fifty states and the District of Columbia. It also includes the report on individual health insurance loopholes in Massachusetts and California, "Coverage When It Counts: How Much Protection Does Health Insurance Offer and How Can Consumers Know?"

Georgetown University Health Policy Institute
3300 Whitehaven Street, NW, Suite 5000
Box 571444
Washington, DC 20057-1485
(202) 687-0880
www.healthinsuranceinfo.net

2

Fixing the Insurance Market

Even people who fought over the rest of the health care bill didn't fight the new rules of the road for the insurance industry. Getting health insurance can be a nightmare when an insurance company can turn you down because you've got a health problem, or raise your rates so much that you have to cancel your coverage, or put in so many hidden loopholes that you're not sure why you're paying all that money in the first place. In other developed countries, they don't let people fall through the cracks like that. And they don't let people go bankrupt because they've gotten sick.

So for all the time Congress spent fighting about abortion or illegal immigrants or "government-run health care," the real point of the health care bill wasn't about any of those things. It was about fixing all of the problems that had made the health insurance companies as popular as swine flu. To get the health care we needed, we had to develop a system that would cover us when we were sick—especially when we were sick—rather than avoiding us when we needed help. It will take a while for the new rules to kick in, but when they do, the hope is that most of the worst practices of the health insurance industry will become a thing of the past.

One of the biggest changes is that health insurance companies won't be able to refuse to cover people with preexisting conditions. That means they can't turn you down based on how healthy you are, what conditions you have, how often you get medical care, what your medical history is, or whether you have a disability, or what kind of injuries you might have. That provision doesn't start for adults until 2014, the year the new health insurance exchanges are supposed to be available in every state. But it starts for kids in September, for all new health plans, since Congress wanted people to see some of the benefits of the new law right away.

This has been one of the hardest problems to solve, especially for people who try to get health insurance on their own. Health insurance companies have been refusing to cover a wide range of conditions, from serious illnesses to common conditions such as asthma and knee injuries. Or, if they covered them, they'd charge much higher premiums than they would charge healthy people. People were mostly protected from this kind of practice if they moved from one job to another and both jobs offered health insurance. But if you left a job to start a business or work on your own, or if you were laid off from your old job, you were in big trouble. That's why Congress thought it was time for the government to step in.

Another big change is that insurance companies will have to accept everyone who applies for health insurance, and they'll have to renew your coverage as long as you want to keep it. This is the way it works in most other industrialized countries. If you sign up for health coverage, they have to take you, and if you have health problems that cost more money than those of other people, they have to figure out other ways to cover those costs. They can't just say no.

But until now, not only have health insurance companies been able to turn people down for just about any health reason, they've also been able to cancel your coverage if you got sick. They could do this if they found any bit of information you left off your health insurance application—no matter how minor. This practice, called "rescissions," will be banned under the new law. In fact, this is one of the first benefits you'll see. Starting in September, rescissions will be illegal for all health plans.

Of course, it would be easy for health insurance companies to say, "We may have to take you, but we can charge you a lot more if you're sick." But under the new law, that's going to be a lot harder than it used to be. Starting in 2014, insurance providers won't be able to charge you higher premiums because of your health history. They'll still be able to make you pay more if you're older, but they won't be able to charge you more than three times as much as the cheapest people in your insurance pool. And the only other reasons the premiums can be different are based on where you live, since health care services cost more in some areas than in others, and based on whether you're buying family or individual coverage. They can also charge you more if you smoke.

The catch is, they could just charge everyone higher premiums if they think they've been forced to take on too many people with health problems. It's a good idea to watch over the next few years to see if that happens. But as we'll see in Chapter 3, the new rule that everyone has to get health insurance, including people who don't think they need it, should bring enough healthy people into the pool that it will cancel out any temptation to raise premiums.

Will My Premiums Go Up?

The Congressional Budget Office predicted that most people won't see any difference in their premiums. People who get their health coverage through the workplace probably won't be affected, and that covers about eight out of ten people with health insurance. In the individual insurance market, where people get health coverage on their own, premiums probably will go up—because the benefits will be better. But even there, about half of the people in this market will get subsidies, and those would more than cancel out the cost of the higher premiums.

So, for most people, coverage is likely to be either the same cost or cheaper than it would have been under the old system. And if any health insurance company raises its rates too much between now and 2014, when the new health insurance exchanges begin, they can be barred from selling their insurance in the exchanges. If any of them decides to take a page from Anthem Blue Cross, the insurer that wanted to raise its rates 39 percent in California, they might think again when they realize how much business they would lose.

Finally, there's going to be an end to another practice that has caused terrible problems for the sickest people. By 2014, health insurance companies won't be able to limit how much they'll pay for your coverage in a year, or how much they'll pay over your lifetime. Right now, it's standard practice to have both annual and lifetime limits on your benefits, which can run out quickly if you get seriously ill or injured and need a lot of care. The lifetime benefit limits end immediately, but the annual limits don't end until 2014. Until then, though, they'll be heavily restricted by the Department of Health and Human Services.

The Minimum Benefits Package

Until now, the federal government hasn't gotten very involved in what kinds of benefits you should get from your health care plan. States have passed laws saying your health plan has to cover certain things, but the federal government hasn't taken much of an interest. That's about to change. By the time the new health insurance exchanges are available, the Department of Health and Human Services is supposed to come up with a minimum benefit package that has to be offered by all health plans in the exchanges.

The goal of the new rules is to keep the exchanges from offering those "limited benefit" plans that cause so much trouble, and to make sure there aren't any big gaps in the plans that are offered. The exact package will be determined by Health and Human Services, but the minimum benefits would be:

- Ambulatory services, such as visits to doctors or urgent care clinics
- Emergency services
- Hospitalization
- Maternity and newborn care
- Mental health, substance abuse, and behavioral disorder treatments
- Prescription drugs
- Rehabilitative services
- Preventive and wellness services and chronic disease management
- Pediatric services, including oral and vision care
- Laboratory services

There also will be new standards for what share of the benefits the exchanges have to cover, to make sure the plans in the exchanges all fall into certain categories so you can compare them. The health insurance companies will have to cover at least 60 percent of the costs for bronze-level plans, 70 percent for silver plans, 80 percent for gold plans, and 90 percent for platinum plans. And the plans will have limits on how much they can make you pay out of pocket every year. Starting in 2014, they can't make you spend more than the out-of-pocket limits for health savings accounts. In 2010 those limits are $5,950 for individuals and $11,900 for families, but they probably will be a bit higher by 2014.

These rules should give you some confidence that you'll have the most important services covered. Remember, though, that the more benefits a health plan has to cover, the more it costs. It's not a trade-off that makes anyone happy, but that's how health insurance works. That's why people have been able to cut their premiums with alternatives such as the limited benefit plans, which are cheap because their coverage is so skimpy, and with health savings accounts, which have cheaper premiums because you spend your own money for the first few thousand dollars of services.

If you use a health insurance exchange, you'll still be able to keep your premiums as low as possible by picking the cheapest plan, the bronze plan. If you're under thirty, you may be able to cut your costs even more by getting a catastrophic plan, which doesn't pay for anything—except preventive care and three primary care visits—until you have paid the same out-of-pocket limits people pay for health savings accounts. But if you want coverage that's more generous than that, be prepared to pay higher premiums.

The Appeals Process

As of September 2010, if you sign up for a new health plan, you'll have the right to ask for an external review if your health plan didn't pay for something you believe was supposed to be covered. Only eighteen states allow this now, so the Department of Health and Human Services is supposed to come up with rules for how to do this in the other states. This means you won't be out of luck if you have already appealed to the health plan and they still said no. If you're already in a state that allows this, the rules probably won't change.

The new law also includes a new protection that should avoid unnecessary hassles in the emergency room. As of September 2010, all new health plans will have to let you receive emergency care without getting your insurer's permission first. This is a throwback to some of the managed-care horror stories of the 1990s, when some patients had to fight with their HMOs to pay for their care because they hadn't phoned ahead from the ambulance.

When You Can Expect to See the Changes

There's one big thing to know about the coming changes: You might not see all of them for a while if you already have coverage. Two of the most important ones—ending lifetime limits on coverage and banning insurance companies from cancelling your coverage when you get sick—will apply to you even if you already have coverage, and they will start in 2010. Others, however, will apply only to new health care plans that go into effect after the dates listed here, not to current health care plans.

And some of them don't even apply to all new plans. For example, the new rules requiring health plans to accept everyone who applies and to renew their coverage, and the rules banning insurers from charging more because of people's health status, don't apply if you're in a "self-insured plan." (See Chapter 1). And the minimum benefits package (see p. 28) won't apply to big employers—only to new health plans for individuals and small businesses. The ban on charging more for people's health status won't apply to large companies, either, unless states decide to make those companies eligible for the new health insurance exchanges.

New Health Insurance Protections	Effective Date
Ban on rejecting preexisting conditions:	
• Children	September 23, 2010 (all employer health care plans and new individual market health care plans)
• Adults	January 1, 2014 (all new health care plans and current group plans)
Ban on "rescissions"	September 23, 2010 (all new and current health care plans)
No lifetime limits	September 23, 2010 (all new and current health care plans)
Appeal rights	September 23, 2010 (all new health plans)
Guaranteed issue and renewal	January 1, 2014 (all new health care plans, except self-insured plans)
No charging higher premiums because of health status or gender	January 1, 2014 (all new individual and small group health plans)
No annual limits	January 1, 2014 (all employer health care plans and new individual market health care plans; annual limits will be restricted, but not banned, starting in September 2010)
Minimum benefits package	January 1, 2014 (all new individual and small group health care plans)

What Do You Do If . . .

You Work for a Small Business

If your employer already offers health insurance, they will be able to continue under the old rules for a while. If they decide to look around for new coverage, their premiums should become more stable after some of the changes go into effect, especially when insurance companies can't raise premiums because you or one of your co-workers gets sick. There isn't expected to be a big rise in premiums when the new rules take effect. Overall, though, your employer might be able to find a better deal by looking for health insurance through the new exchanges. That's because the exchanges are supposed to allow small businesses to join larger insurance "pools" so everyone's health care costs are spread out among more people. See Chapter 6 for more information.

You Work for a Medium-Size or Large Company

Even if your employer already offers health insurance, they will have to give you most of the important new protections, including the ban on lifetime limits. Any waiting periods you would have faced for preexisting conditions (if you're a new employee and haven't had group coverage for a while) should be gone, too. You already had more protections than people getting health insurance on their own—the health insurer can't reject you for coverage or completely refuse to cover a preexisting condition.

If you work for a "self-insured" company, which takes on all of the financial risk for health coverage, you won't get some of the new protections—such as the ban on raising premiums because of a person's health status or the minimum benefits package (see p. 28).

You Have Individual Health Insurance

Your current health plan won't have to comply with all of the new rules. But starting in September 2010, you will be able to take advantage of some of the new protections: the ban on cancelling coverage when you get sick and the ban on lifetime limits for your coverage. If you have children and you apply for new individual coverage after September 2010, the insurance company won't be able to reject your children for preexisting conditions. You won't get the full set of protections, however, until 2014. And since one of the most important ones—requiring insurance companies to accept you if you apply—doesn't kick in until then, you shouldn't cancel your old individual insurance until you know you've been accepted into a new plan.

You're Uninsured

The new protections should make it a lot easier for you to find health coverage, as long as the new rules don't raise premiums too much. And even if they do, there will be subsidies available to soften the blow. The Congressional Budget Office, which studies all bills like this to predict their costs, believes that the new protections will make premiums a bit more expensive. But it also believes that more than half of the new people who sign up for health coverage will get the subsidies, and that the subsidies will more than make up for the higher premiums. (See Chapter 4.)

If you apply this year, some of the big rules will be in effect: the ban on cancelling coverage when you get sick and the ban on lifetime limits for your coverage. And if you have children, the insurance company won't be able to reject them for preexisting conditions. But the rest won't start until 2014, and that includes one of the biggest ones: requiring insurance companies to accept you if you apply. So there might be a rough period, between now and 2014, when insurance companies have to comply with some of the new rules but don't have to accept you. Once they have to accept you, and neither adults nor children can be rejected for preexisting conditions, you should have an easier time.

You're on Medicare

The new rules don't apply to you, since they're meant for people in the private insurance market.

You're on Medicaid

The new rules don't apply to you, since they're meant for people in the private insurance market.

You Have a Child in the State Children's Health Insurance Program

The new rules don't apply to you, since they're meant for people in the private insurance market.

You're an Early Retiree, Age Fifty-Five to Sixty-Four

If you have health insurance, your current plan doesn't have to follow the new rules. If you want to switch, or if you've been dropped from the retiree health coverage you used to have, you will get some of the new protections right away, but the biggest ones won't kick in until 2014. These include the new rules requiring insurance companies to accept anyone who applies, banning insurers from rejecting you if you have a preexisting condition, and banning them from charging you higher premiums because of your health. They will be able to charge you more than other customers because of your age, but they won't be able to charge you more than three times as much as the cheapest customers.

In the meantime, there will be temporary risk pools available to cover you if you have a preexisting condition and can't wait until all of the new rules are in effect. See Chapter 8 for more information.

You Are Under Age

There's a new rule that might make it easier for young adults to get cheap coverage. Starting this year, you'll be able to stay on your parents' health insurance as dependents until you turn twenty-six. It may not be something you'll want to brag about, but being a dependent in a family health insurance policy may be cheaper than getting health coverage on your own—and it could be a good option if you're working at a starting job that doesn't offer health insurance. And starting in 2014, you can also get catastrophic health coverage if you're under thirty or if you can't afford the other health plans available through the new health insurance exchanges.

In September 2010, young adults under age 26 will be able to be covered as dependents on their parents' health insurance. They can be added to any existing group or individual health plan that allows dependent coverage.

3

Everyone Has to Have Health Coverage

Surprise! It's not okay to be uninsured anymore. One of the biggest changes the new health care law makes, which will affect millions of Americans, is that everyone will soon be required to have health coverage. If you really can't afford it, and can prove it, you'll be able to get an exemption. But most people will have to have coverage of some kind, whether it's through the workplace, an individual health insurance policy, Medicare or Medicaid, or military or Veterans Administration health insurance. The new rule: Get yourself covered, or come up with a really good reason why you can't.

It might sound like a harsh policy, and it is facing legal challenges that will try to stop it before it even gets going. But the "individual mandate," as it is called, has come to be accepted by many policymakers as the only way to get most uninsured people into the system. Many people are uninsured because they truly can't afford health coverage. Most of them are working adults who earn just a bit too much to qualify for the Medicaid program for low-income people. And it has never been as easy as it should be to sign up for public programs such as

Medicaid and the State Children's Health Insurance Program. But a lot of uninsured people are also relatively young and healthy, so it may not be a big priority for them to spend money on health insurance, especially if it's expensive.

The problem, though, is that when uninsured people need health care and can't pay for it, the costs get spread to everyone else. And when healthy people don't sign up for coverage, they aren't paying the premiums that help to keep other people's costs down. Remember, the more health problems there are in the "pool" of insured people, the more expensive everyone's coverage is. If you can get more healthy people into the pool, you have a better chance at stabilizing everyone's costs.

In 2009, to cover the costs of treating uninsured people, Americans paid an average of $410 in individual insurance premiums and $1,100 in family premiums, according to a study by the Center for American Progress Action Fund. That's about 8 percent of the average health insurance premium.

The individual mandate is the answer to years of failure in trying to expand health coverage in small steps. Think of it as the health care version of the way we treat car insurance. We don't let drivers decide whether to get car insurance. Everyone has to have it, as a way to keep the cost of accidents down for everyone else. If we treat car insurance this way, the argument went, why should we treat health insurance as less important? Such a mandate is also common for the other industrialized countries that have covered all of their citizens.

We already have an example in the United States of how an individual mandate can work. It's in Massachusetts, where the 2006 health care law requires everyone to have health insurance, except for children and adults whose income is less than 150 percent of the federal poverty line. (In 2010, that's $16,245 a year for individuals, and $33,075 a year for a family of four.) Massachusetts residents can also get a "certificate of exemption" if they have other kinds of financial problems, such as getting evicted or having their utilities cut off, or if paying health insurance would make it hard for them to afford basic things such as food, shelter, or clothing.

There is also a political reason for the individual mandate: It was the price President Obama and Congress had to pay to keep the health insurance industry from using its political power to oppose the bill. Whenever people criticized health insurance companies for all of their unsavory practices, such as denying coverage for preexisting conditions and raising premiums sky high when people got sick, the insurance companies would respond that they had to use those practices because healthy people delayed signing up for health coverage until they needed it. If they had a guarantee that healthy people would be in the system, they said, they could drop the worst of their practices.

Forcing people to get coverage, however, is a big step, and one that raises all sorts of difficult questions. How much are people going to have to pay for health insurance? How much is going to be done to make it cheaper? How much will the penalty be for not complying? And how big of a financial hit will the new mandate be for people who are already struggling to earn enough money to live? These problems are serious enough that Obama only reluctantly agreed to support the idea. In fact, as a presidential candidate, he opposed it, arguing that people don't choose to be uninsured, and that if they could afford health insurance, they would get it. He changed his mind after taking office, but only after his health care advisers insisted it would be the only way to come close to the goal of health coverage for all Americans. And he said the health care bill would have to include a way for people to get hardship exemptions if they really couldn't afford the coverage.

The new law does have hardship exemptions in it, and subsidies to help people with modest incomes pay for health insurance. We'll explore those subsidies in the next chapter. And Medicaid is going to expand in the next few years, so that by the time everyone has to have health coverage, it will be a better option for people who don't earn a lot of money. But Congress could do only so much to help people pay for coverage, because it was trying to hold down the costs of the health care bill. And if you decide health insurance is too expensive and Congress doesn't think you're poor enough, you will have to pay a penalty.

When the Senate was debating the bill, Republican senator John Ensign of Nevada tried to argue that the individual mandate was unconstitutional in two ways: Congress didn't have the power to make that kind of rule, and it violated the Fifth Amendment's ban on taking private property for public purposes "without just compensation." He lost the argument, and the Senate defeated his challenge to the rule. But if there's any question about whether the individual mandate is constitutional, you can bet it will be explored at length in the legal challenges that lie ahead.

What Will You Have to Pay?

Premiums

The new health care law helps out with subsidies until your income has reached four times the federal poverty line. In 2010, that's $43,320 for an individual, and $88,200 for a family of four. That's well above the mid-range of what most people earn in the United States. But when you've reached that level, you might have to pay as much as 9.5 percent of your annual income in premiums. So an individual earning $45,000 would have to pay as much as $4,275 a year in premiums, while a family of four earning $90,000 might have to pay $8,550 a year.

This depends on what kind of plan you choose, though, and you could lower your premiums by picking a plan with less generous benefits. And the less you earn, the more help you'll get. (See Chapter 4 for a better breakdown of what you might have to pay at different income levels.)

Out-of-Pocket Costs

Another important factor, besides the premiums, is how much you might have to pay in out-of-pocket costs. Remember that these include your coinsurance and deductible payments, and sometimes your routine co-payments (check the fine print), but they don't include premiums. Under the new law, you're not supposed to pay more than $5,950 for individuals and $11,900 for families in out-of-pocket costs—though, of course, that's still a lot of money for anybody. People with lower incomes will get help with that, too. You'll have to pay only a third of those amounts if you earn less than twice the federal poverty level, for example, and you'll gradually pay more as your income rises. (See Chapter 4 for a better illustration of how this would work.)

What Is the Penalty If You Don't Sign Up?

The new coverage rules will be enforced through the tax code, and you know what that means: The IRS will be watching you. Your employer (or whoever else provides your health coverage) will have to report what kind of health coverage you have. If it's your employer, for example, they will file a return that includes your name, your address, your taxpayer identification number, the dates you had health coverage, and how much of the premium the employer paid. They also have to send you a notice letting you know what they've told the IRS.

As long as your plan is one of the acceptable kinds of coverage, you'll be fine. If it's not, or you have no health coverage at all, you'll have to pay a penalty: either a flat fee for each uninsured person or a percentage of your income, whichever is greater. Here is how the penalties would be phased in over the coming years, and what you would pay under either version:

Effective Date	Flat Fee
2014	$95
2015	$325
2016	$695
After 2016	Indexed for inflation
Maximum penalty for a family	$2,085

Date	Percentage of Income
2014	1
2015	2
2016 and beyond	2.5

There are a lot of different kinds of coverage that would satisfy the new rules. Besides coverage through the workplace or through the new health insurance exchanges, you will be considered insured if you have Medicare or Medicaid coverage, if your children are enrolled in the State Children's Health Insurance Program, if you're in the military and get coverage through TRICARE, or you're a veteran and get it through the Veterans Administration. If you already have coverage through the workplace or through individual insurance, that should count as well.

Who's Exempt?

The new law lets you off the hook if you really can't find coverage you can afford. For example, if your only health insurance options would make you spend more than 8 percent of your income on premiums, you should be able to get an exemption. You also won't face any penalty if you are uninsured for less than three months, if you're a member of a Native American tribe, or if you earn too little to owe any taxes. (In 2009, individuals who earned less than $9,350 and married couples who made less than $18,700 didn't have to file a tax return.) In order to avoid the penalty, you'd apply for a certificate of exemption from your state's health insurance exchange, which will send the IRS the names of everyone who doesn't have to have health insurance.

In Massachusetts, where they already have an individual mandate, they have made it work by developing a new tax form where people report what kind of health insurance they have. All but about 2 percent of people who filed taxes in Massachusetts for 2008 filed the form, and most state residents—about 98 percent—had health coverage at some point during the year. Only a little more than 1 percent of Massachusetts taxpayers who could have afforded health insurance didn't have it.

What Do You Do If . . .

You Work for a Small Business

Your employer may or may not be able to give you the kind of health insurance you need. They'll be able to get a tax credit for two years, and that might make it easier for them to provide health coverage. But if they can't, you will have to look for coverage through the new insurance exchanges, which start in 2014, the same year that the new coverage requirement begins. You can also use the health insurance exchanges if your employer is offering you health insurance, but you'd have to pay more than 9.5 percent of your annual income for it because your employer won't pay enough of your premium. (See Chapter 6 for more about the exchanges.)

You Work for a Medium-Size or Large Company

Employers are supposed to either give you health coverage or pay a fee if they don't—but only if they have more than fifty workers. If they're already giving you coverage, whatever they're giving you is likely to satisfy the rules. If you're in one of those "limited benefit" plans, you'll be able to stay in it. You just won't be able to sign up for new ones starting in 2014.

If your employer doesn't have to give you coverage because they don't have enough workers, or they offer it but you'd have to pay more than 9.5 percent of your annual income for it, or if they choose to pay the fee instead, you might need to look for coverage in the health insurance exchanges. The exchanges will be available in 2014, the same year that the new coverage requirement begins. (See Chapter 6.)

You Have Individual Health Insurance

Your current insurance should satisfy the new coverage rules. If you're trying to buy individual insurance for the first time or to improve what you've got, the health insurance exchanges won't be available until the new coverage requirement kicks in, in 2014. However, some new rules should make it easier for you to get coverage in the meantime. These are described in more detail in Chapter 8, but here's a brief rundown:

- There will be a new, temporary high-risk pool to cover people who haven't been able to get health insurance because they have preexisting conditions that the insurance companies consider too expensive. It will be run through the states, and most likely, states that already have these kinds of high-risk pools will be able to continue them. Unfortunately, high-risk pools aren't always the best solution. Many of them charge high premiums because everyone in them has health problems—or they scale back their coverage levels to keep the premiums from rising too high—and some states have to limit enrollment because they'd run out of money otherwise. Still, until the new exchanges begin and insurers stop being able to reject you for preexisting conditions, this might be an option to consider. The risk pool is supposed to end when the exchanges begin, in 2014, but a word of warning: They might stop taking new people if the funds run out before then. Check your state insurance agency Web site through the National Association of Insurance Commissioners interactive map, at www.naic .org/state_web_map.htm.

- Remember that health insurance companies are supposed to end the practice of "rescissions"—cancelling people's coverage retroactively because they left out something on their application for health insurance. So that's one less thing you have to worry about. They're also supposed to stop putting limits on what they'll pay out over your lifetime, and they will be restricted as to the limits they can place on what they pay out in any given year. And children can't be turned down anymore for having preexisting conditions.

- By July 1, 2010, the Department of Health and Human Services is supposed to set up a new Web site to help you look for affordable health insurance options. It won't list the "limited benefit" plans, so you're less likely to get stuck with inadequate health insurance. Until that is up and running, eHealthInsurance.com is a good private alternative. They'll help you search for coverage only among their health insurance partners, but they have a lot of partnerships.

You're Uninsured

You have until 2014 to get insured. The exchanges will be available that year, and will likely be your best way to find health insurance at group rates. In the meantime, if you can't get into a private health insurance plan because of a preexisting condition, try the temporary risk pool, which is supposed to start this year. The new Department of Health and Human Services Web site should be able to help you search for options. You can also run a quick search on eHealthInsurance.com. See the section "You Have Individual Health Insurance."

If your income is low enough, you should also check with your state Medicaid office. Starting in 2014, the program is supposed to expand to cover more people, including those with incomes up to 133 percent of the federal poverty line and low-income adults without children. Some states might start expanding their programs before then. So it's worth checking to see what's happening in your state. Check the appendix for the phone number and Web site in your state.

A couple of things to watch out for: Health insurance companies still have a lot of freedom to raise premiums, and they might do so before the new rules on premium rates kick in. Starting in 2014, they won't be able to charge you higher premiums because of your health status, and there will be other limits on what they can do. But until those rules take effect, everyone will be watching to see if the insurers start raising everyone's premiums while they still can. They're supposed to justify any premium increases to the new health insurance exchanges and post their explanations on their Web sites. So it might be worth checking the insurers' Web sites, and the new Department of Health and Human Services site, to watch for this. Also, if you sign up for health insurance now, watch out for those "limited benefit" plans. They're not supposed to be available through the exchanges, but they're still available now.

You're on Medicare

You don't have to do anything. Your coverage will satisfy the new rules.

You're on Medicaid

You don't have to do anything. Your coverage will satisfy the new rules.

You Have a Child in the State Children's Health Insurance Program

As long as you keep them enrolled, their coverage will satisfy the rules.

You're an Early Retiree, Age Fifty-Five to Sixty-Four

If you have health insurance through your former employer, you should be fine as long as they don't cancel their retiree health benefits. There's going to be a temporary "reinsurance" program that might make it easier for them to maintain your coverage. It's supposed to reimburse them for expensive health care, and in turn, they're supposed to pass on the savings to you in some way—such as by lowering premiums, copayments, or deductibles. (See Chapter 8 for more information.) But this program ends when the exchanges begin, or sooner, if the money runs out before then.

4

Getting Help Paying for Coverage

If everyone has to have health coverage, the next link in the chain is to help people who would have trouble paying for it. Lots of people would fit that description, of course, and there's only so much federal money available to help. (Insert your favorite bailout joke here.) Still, it's important to know that if your income is low enough, you can apply for a tax credit that might take some of the sting out of the cost of health coverage. And if you're a small business owner trying to do the right thing for your workers, there's a tax credit that might help you, too.

When Congress was writing the health care bill, lawmakers knew they had to make health insurance more affordable for people if they were going to make everyone get it. Since President Obama was never a big fan of forcing people to get health coverage, he insisted on providing subsidies for the people who would take the biggest financial hit. The easiest way to do that is through tax credits, which can give you back some of the money you've spent on health insurance. The members of Congress who wrote the bill decided they had enough money to help people with incomes up to four times the federal poverty line. Right now, that's $43,320 for an individual and $88,200 for a family of four.

So, starting in 2014, the first year you're required to get health coverage, there will be a tax credit that can help you pay your premiums, and you'll also be eligible for cost-sharing subsidies to limit the amount of money you have to spend out of pocket for your health care. The assistance starts out big for the poorest people, and then becomes smaller as you earn more money, phasing out when you reach four times the federal poverty line. There will also be an extra layer of help for low-income people, as health plans will have to pick up a bigger share of the costs of your benefits.

How the Subsidies Will Work

For an Individual

Income: $14,404
Percentage of federal poverty level: 133 percent*
Maximum annual premium: $288 (2 percent of annual income)
Out-of-pocket limit: $1,983 (one third of standard limit)†
Cost-sharing: Health plan pays 94 percent of costs

---

*Based on 2010 federal poverty guidelines for individuals.

†Based on 2010 out-of-pocket limit for health savings accounts.

Income: $16,245
Percentage of federal poverty level: 150 percent
Maximum annual premium: $650 (4 percent)
Out-of-pocket limit: $1,983 (one third of standard limit)
Cost-sharing: Health plan pays 94 percent

Income: $21,660
Percentage of federal poverty level: 200 percent
Maximum annual premium: $1,365 (6.3 percent)
Out-of-pocket limit: $1,983 (one third of standard limit)
Cost-sharing: Health plan pays 87 percent

Income: $27,075
Percentage of federal poverty level: 250 percent
Maximum annual premium: $2,180 (8.05 percent)
Out-of-pocket limit: $2,975 (half the standard limit)
Cost-sharing: Health plan pays 73 percent

Income: $32,490
Percentage of federal poverty level: 300 percent
Maximum annual premium: $3,087 (9.5 percent)
Out-of-pocket limit: $2,975 (half the standard limit)
Cost-sharing: Health plan pays 70 percent

Income: $43,320
Percentage of federal poverty level: 400 percent
Maximum annual premium: $4,115 (9.5 percent)
Out-of-pocket limit: $3,967 (two thirds of the standard limit)
Cost-sharing: Health plan pays 70 percent

For a Family of Four

Income: $29,327
Percentage of federal poverty level: 133 percent*
Maximum annual premium: $587 (2 percent of annual income)
Out-of-pocket limit: $3,967 (one third of standard limit)
Cost-sharing: Health plan pays 94 percent

Income: $33,075
Percentage of federal poverty level: 150 percent
Maximum annual premium: $1,323 (4 percent)
Out-of-pocket limit: $3,967 (one third of standard limit)
Cost-sharing: Health plan pays 94 percent

Income: $44,100
Percentage of federal poverty level: 200 percent
Maximum annual premium: $2,778 (6.3 percent)
Out-of-pocket limit: $3,967 (one third of standard limit)
Cost-sharing: Health plan pays 87 percent

Income: $55,125
Percentage of federal poverty level: 250 percent
Maximum annual premium: $4,438 (8.05 percent)
Out-of-pocket limit: $5,950 (half the standard limit)
Cost-sharing: Health plan pays 73 percent

---

*Based on 2010 federal poverty guidelines for a family of four.

Income: $66,150
Percentage of federal poverty level: 300 percent
Maximum annual premium: $6,284 (9.5 percent)
Out-of-pocket limit: $5,950 (half the standard limit)
Cost-sharing: Health plan pays 70 percent

Income: $88,200
Percentage of federal poverty level: 400 percent
Maximum annual premium: $8,379 (9.5 percent)
Out-of-pocket limit: $7,933 (two thirds of the standard limit)
Cost-sharing: Health plan pays 70 percent

It's important to note that a health plan that covers 70 percent of the costs doesn't necessarily cover 70 percent of *your* costs. That's an average for everyone in your health plan, assuming they're an average group of people. Your own costs might be higher or lower, depending on how often you use the health care system. For a more detailed explanation of how this works, see Chapter 6.

If you're living from paycheck to paycheck, it may still seem like you'll have to pay a lot of money for health insurance. Members of Congress did talk a lot about how much help people should get, but they had limits on how much they could spend on subsidies. That's because Obama wanted a bill that paid for itself, and wouldn't add to the deficit by the end of ten years. He also wanted a bill that wouldn't cost more than $900 billion, before you counted all of the cuts in other areas that would be used to pay for it. So whatever Congress did to help people with modest incomes, they had to keep it within those limits. House and Senate Democrats argued over how much help people should get at different income levels, and this was the best compromise they could come up with.

How the Subsidies Work

You would get two different forms of assistance: a tax credit to reduce your premiums, and a separate cost-sharing credit that would bring down your total out-of-pocket expenses and reduce the amount of the plan's costs that you would have to pay. The tax credit is to be used in the new health insurance exchanges, and it's mainly for people who can't get health coverage through the workplace. However, you can also use it if your employer provides health coverage but covers less than 60 percent of your costs, or if you would have to pay more than 9.5 percent of your income for coverage.

There would be a bit of a bureaucracy to deal with in order to get your credits. The Department of Health and Human Services would have to determine if you were eligible, and if you were, it would then inform the Treasury Department and the health insurance exchange in your state. Then the Treasury Department would pay your tax credit directly to your health insurance company. Finally, the insurance company would reduce your premium. There would be a way to get the credits paid in advance, possibly every month. The process would be similar for your cost-sharing reductions.

There's one important bit of fine print about the tax credit: It won't count toward any extra benefits that your state requires all health insurance plans to cover. So if health insurance is unusually expensive in your state, because the state makes health plans cover more things than you would get under the new federal law, the tax credit might not help you as much as it would in other states.

How to Apply for the Subsidies

You'll be able to apply for the premium tax credit and the cost-sharing credit through the new health insurance exchanges when you first sign up for coverage. When you apply, you'll fill out your name, address, date of birth, and Social Security number, and report your income and family size. You'll also have to report your citizenship or immigration status, since people who are in the country illegally can't buy health coverage through the exchanges, even with their own money.

To prove that you're eligible for the help, you'll have to supply information from the tax return you filed two years before the year you're applying to get coverage. So if you're applying for the tax credit in 2014, for example—the first year it's available—you would report information from your 2012 tax return. If you have unpredictable income or have just become unemployed, there should be procedures for dealing with that, such as letting you estimate what your income will be. But these are not spelled out in the new law, so the federal agencies concerned will have to figure them out later.

It's a lot for the bureaucracies to keep track of, and you might think it's a recipe for fraud. But anyone who lies about their income or any other information to get bigger subsidies, and gets caught, could face a fine of up to $250,000. If it's a simple mistake, they could still be on the hook for a $25,000 fine.

The Small Business Tax Credit

The other group Congress wanted to help with the cost of health insurance is small businesses. There's a good reason for that. Small businesses have been struggling with the rising cost of health insurance more than any other employers. They have been paying about 18 percent more than other employers for the same kind of health insurance, and their struggles are a big reason why people have been losing coverage. In 2008, fewer than four out of ten small businesses provided health insurance, compared with six out of ten in 1993.

So the new law has a second set of tax credits aimed at small businesses, to make it easier for them to cover their workers. Starting in tax year 2010, any small businesses with up to twenty-five full-time employees and average wages of up to $50,000 a year will be able to get a credit for up to 35 percent of the premiums if they provide health coverage. And in 2014 the credit will get bigger, covering up to 50 percent of the premiums. Only the smallest businesses will get the full credit—the ones with up to ten full-time employees and average wages of up to $25,000 a year—and the others will get slightly less.

If you need more technical information about the small business tax credit, the Joint Committee on Taxation has an in-depth analysis available on its Web site, www.jct.gov. You can also use it to learn more about how the premium tax credits and cost-sharing subsidies will work.

You'll find the technical explanation under the release date, March 21, 2010, and its publication number, JCX-18-10. The section on the small business tax credit starts on page 26. You'll find the section on the premium tax credits starting on page 10, and the explanation of the cost-sharing subsidies starting on page 18.

Unfortunately, small businesses can't count on the tax credit forever. Once the full credit begins in 2014, they'll be able to get it for only two years, thanks to budget constraints. But the way Congress works, you can expect lobbyists for small businesses to demand that the tax credit be extended beyond those two years, and they just might succeed. And for now, small business owners will be able to count on at least six years of tax credits, and the new health insurance exchanges are supposed to help them join together in bigger insurance "pools" so their costs will be more stable. That may be enough, at least for a while, to stop the trend of small businesses dropping their employees' health coverage.

The New Tax Credits

For individuals: January 1, 2014

For small businesses: The first phase starts in 2010. Small businesses will be able to get a tax credit for up to 35 percent of their contribution to the premium. Tax-exempt businesses get 25 percent. In the second phase, which starts in 2014, they can get a credit for up to 50 percent for two years if they get their health insurance through the new health insurance exchanges. Tax-exempt businesses will get up to 35 percent.

What Do You Do If . . .

You Work for a Small Business

Bug your boss to apply for the small business tax credit. It can't hurt, and it might make it easier for the business to keep offering health insurance—or to start offering it if it doesn't already. Be aware, though, that the tax credit can do only so much to help a small business. The business can get it for a total of only six years, it's aimed mainly at the smallest of small businesses, and it doesn't address all of the root causes of the rapid growth in health care spending.

The health insurance exchanges may be able to provide more help by allowing small businesses to join larger insurance pools so their premiums aren't affected so much by how many people get sick. In the long term, though, small businesses will be able to keep offering health insurance only if we can keep overall health care spending from growing so fast. And that will happen only if some of the experiments in the new law, aimed at changing how we pay for health care, show some real success in bringing down costs. See Chapter 14 for more on these experiments.

You Work for a Medium-Size or Large Company

Remember that you might be able to get a subsidy even if your employer already offers health insurance—if your plan pays less than 60 percent of the costs of your care, or if your share would be more than 9.5 percent of your annual income. And you definitely can get a subsidy if your company doesn't offer health insurance.

The big unknown, though, is whether you could apply for the tax credit without getting in trouble with your employer. If you get the credit, your company pays a fine (described in Chapter 5). The law bans your company from retaliating against you by paying you less or punishing you in some other direct way, and you'll be able to file a complaint if it does. But even though most employers will be smart enough not to retaliate against you directly, there are all kinds of ways they can apply more subtle pressure to discourage you from applying. If you think your employer is steering you away from asking for the tax credit, contact your nearest regional office of the Department of Labor's Employee Benefits Security Administration. You can find the one in your area by calling 1-866-444-3272.

There's also a chance that some companies might prefer that you get your health insurance through an exchange. If they think it will cost them less to pay the fine than to give you health coverage, that's what they might do. Each employer will make the decision based on what makes the most economic sense for them, but they'll also consider what they have to do to attract the best workers. They might not have to offer health benefits now, as long as the economy is bad and people are out of work, but the economy won't stay bad forever.

You Have Individual Health Insurance

Even if you already have individual coverage, you might want to consider switching to a plan offered through the new health insurance exchanges. That will make you eligible for the subsidy starting in 2014, the first year the exchanges will be available. One thing to keep in mind is that the premium tax credit is calculated based on the second-lowest cost "silver" plan in your area (the kind that covers 70 percent of the costs). If you use it on one of the more generous plans—such as the "gold" or "platinum" plan—the tax credit might not be worth as much. Still, it could make your individual coverage a bit less expensive than it is now, if your income is low enough.

You're Uninsured

The subsidies are meant to help you get health insurance. If you earn less than four times the federal poverty level—$43,320 for an individual in 2010—you should be able to use the tax credit to get coverage through a health insurance exchange, starting in 2014. If you earn more than that, Congress believes you should be able to afford health insurance on your own.

Remember, though, that Congress put into the new law only as much in subsidies as they thought they could afford. If your subsidy is not enough for you, and you're still struggling with the cost of health insurance once you've gotten it, let your senator or local member of Congress know about it. You can find a listing of senators and their contact information on the official Senate Web site, www.senate.gov, and there's a "Write Your Representative" link on the official House site, www.house .gov. There are also privately run Web sites that let you find your elected officials by typing in your zip code. Two of the main ones are Congress .org (www.congress.org) and Project Vote Smart (www.votesmart.org).

And if all else fails, there's always the option of paying the fine and not getting health insurance. Before choosing that option, though, think about the kind of risk you're taking in case you do get a serious illness or injury, no matter how healthy you are now. One bad turn of events could wipe you out. And remember that if you can't pay your bills, everyone else pays them for you. That's one of the reasons health insurance has gotten so expensive in the first place.

You're on Medicare

Sorry. The subsidies are intended only for private insurance.

You're on Medicaid

The subsidies don't apply to you.

You Have a Child in the State Children's Health Insurance Program

The subsidies don't apply to you.

You're an Early Retiree, Age Fifty-Five to Sixty-Four

The tax credit could be part of your ticket to getting health insurance if you don't have it or if your employer has dropped your retiree coverage. It applies only to coverage you get through the new health insurance exchanges, so that will be your best option—especially since the exchange plans will also have all the new protections that should make it easier for you to get accepted for coverage.

If you do have retiree coverage but you're struggling with the costs, it might be worth your while to check out the exchange plans when they're available, starting in 2014. They might be less expensive than your current coverage, depending on what's available and how much of a subsidy you'd get. Keep in mind that individual health insurance will be more expensive for you than for other people, even in the exchanges. But the subsidies might take some of the edge off the costs.

5

What Employers Have to Do

The new health care law is built around a concept of "shared responsibility." That means you, your employer, and the government all have to do things to make sure everyone gets health coverage. Your job is to get yourself covered. The government's job—at the national level, but also at the state levels—is to make it easier for you to do that. And your employer's job is to give you health coverage if that's at all possible. If they can't afford it, or just choose not to do it, their job is to pay a fee that can help you get the coverage you need elsewhere.

Starting in 2014, employers throughout the country will be expected to live up to their end of this bargain. Congress wrestled with this issue, because it's not clear how far you can go to make businesses offer health coverage without hurting the workers in other ways. If health coverage is too expensive for businesses that aren't doing all that well, they might not hire as many people, or they might not pay as much for the jobs they do have. Some of them might even go out of business. It's hard to know how much of this threat is real and how much of it was exaggerated by the groups who didn't want the health care bill to pass.

But everyone in Congress knew that there was at least a small possibility that the new health coverage rules could backfire.

The answer they came up with was to make employers pay a fee if they didn't cover their workers, but not actually require them to provide health coverage. That was a way to take some of the sting out of the new rules, and perhaps make sure business groups didn't fight the health care bill quite as hard. The idea of making all businesses provide health coverage—an "employer mandate"—has been around since the last time Congress tried to expand health coverage to all Americans, under President Bill Clinton. That effort failed for a lot of reasons, but one of the big ones was the opposition of business groups.

This time, President Obama and key members of Congress tried harder to get the business groups on board. Some of the most powerful groups still fought the bill, but the business community was more divided this time than it was in the 1990s. They knew that whatever problems they had with the new law, sticking with the old system wasn't the answer. The old system was eating into their bottom line, and their workers' paychecks, as health care premiums increased much faster than inflation. The new system will have to do better at getting those costs under control, and as we'll see in Chapter 14, we won't know for a while whether its experiments are working. But if everyone is covered, with the help of businesses, that's at least one step toward making the system more stable.

There never has been a rule that businesses have to provide health coverage. That's just how our system has evolved since World War II. At the time, businesses were under wage and price controls and couldn't attract workers by offering to pay them high salaries. So they started offering health insurance as a fringe benefit, as a way of getting around the pay limits. Since then, most of us have become used to getting health insurance through the workplace, with our employers paying most of the costs. About six out of ten Americans get health coverage from their employers.

The system works well for those of us who get generous coverage, mainly at medium-size to large companies. It works less well for those of us who work for low-wage shops or retail chains that have tried to skimp on health care benefits or that don't offer them at all. And businesses have cut back on health insurance since 2000, when seven out of ten Americans had coverage through the workplace. Still, we're used to the employment-based system, and it does provide big advantages. Employers pay most of the premiums, and we don't get taxed on the benefits. You miss those advantages when you don't have them. So if we were going to come close to the goal of covering all Americans, Congress knew that employers had to be a big part of the solution.

How the New Rules Will Work

If any business with more than fifty full-time workers doesn't offer health insurance, and any of its employees gets the tax credit to help them get coverage through the new health insurance exchanges, that business will have to pay a fine of $2,000 for every full-time worker they have—though they won't be charged for the first thirty workers. This way, the smaller businesses would be shielded from at least some of the penalty, so they would have less of an incentive to keep their number of workers under fifty. (Any employer with fifty or fewer employees is exempt from the fine.)

The Treasury Department will decide how the fine should be paid, probably in the form of a tax penalty. Here's how it would affect businesses of different sizes: If you work at a business with fifty-one employees and it doesn't offer health insurance, it would be charged for twenty-one of the workers—so it would pay a fine of $42,000. On the other hand, a business with a hundred employees that didn't offer health coverage would be charged for seventy workers, so its total fine would be $140,000.

There is also a different penalty for any employer that offers coverage that's too expensive for their workers. If they offer health coverage, but any one of their employees gets the tax credit, the company will have to pay either $2,000 for every full-time employee or $3,000 for each worker who receives the subsidy—whichever is less.

In general, if your company offers health coverage, you have to take it. You won't be able to use the new health insurance exchanges. But there are exceptions to this rule. If they offer coverage that covers less than 60 percent of the costs, or would make you pay more than 9.5 percent of your annual income, you would be able to get the subsidy and go to the exchange because your employer's coverage would be considered too expensive—and they would have to pay the penalty.

There's also an exception that allows you to take the money your employer pays for health coverage and use it at an exchange instead. If you have to pay more than 8 percent, but less than 9.5 percent, of your annual income for your company's health insurance—meaning you wouldn't be expected to have health coverage, but you would qualify for the tax subsidy—you can ask your employer for a "free choice voucher," which would let you use the employer's money to get health coverage through an exchange. This applies only if you earn less than four times the federal poverty level—$43,320 for as individual, and $88,200 for a family of four. There's no penalty for the employer if you use the voucher, since it's their money and that means they're still contributing to your health care.

Your employer is also expected to make it as easy as possible for you to sign up for coverage. If you're at a company with more than two hundred full-time workers, the company is supposed to enroll new workers automatically into one of their health plans. They have to give you a heads-up that they're doing this, and they have to give you a chance to cancel your enrollment if you don't want the coverage—or to switch to one of their other plans if that's not the one you want.

If your employer offers a health plan that covers less than 60 percent of your costs, or would make you pay more than 9.5 percent of your annual income, it will be considered too expensive for you. So, starting in 2014, if you want to try to cut your costs, you can apply for a subsidy and get your health coverage through your state's health insurance exchange instead.

Finally, the new law requires your employer to tell you about the options you'll have with the health insurance exchanges: that the exchanges exist, once the exchanges are ready, and that you can get your health coverage through the exchanges instead of through the workplace if your employer's health plan would cover less than 60 percent of your costs. They'll also have to warn you, however, that if you get your coverage through an exchange, you'll lose the amount the employer would have paid for your health insurance—unless you're in the category that qualifies you for one of the "free choice vouchers."

Change	Effective Date
New Employer Rules	January 1, 2014

What Do You Do If . . .

You Work for a Small Business

The new coverage rules are aimed at larger companies, not small businesses. So if you work for a business that has fifty employees or fewer, your chances of getting health coverage through the workplace probably won't change. They're more likely to be affected by whether the new health insurance exchanges make it easier for your employer to find coverage it can afford, and whether the small business tax credit will give it enough help paying for the coverage.

It is possible that small businesses with mostly young and healthy workers will be more likely to offer coverage, according to the Congressional Budget Office, which studies the costs of bills passed by Congress. That's because the tax credit—and the new rule that everyone must have health insurance—will make it more likely that those businesses will get the coverage rather than skipping it.

You Work for a Medium-Size or Large Company

This part of the new law is aimed at your company. If you have health insurance already, and it's not too expensive for you, you probably won't see a big difference. But if your plan makes you pay more than 60 percent of the costs, or 9.5 percent of your annual income, you'll be able to go to a health insurance exchange to look for a better deal, and your employer will be fined. That's not likely, though, because most large companies' health plans already cover more than 60 percent of the costs. You will notice a change once companies start automatically enrolling new workers into the cheapest plans.

If your company doesn't offer health insurance, it will have to make an economic decision about whether to start offering it or pay the fine. And, honestly, it would cost the company a lot less to pay the fine than to offer the coverage. In 2009 the average premium for employer-based health plans was $4,824 for single coverage and $13,375 for family coverage, according to the Henry J. Kaiser Family Foundation. Even though an employer isn't going to pay all of that amount—you'll pay part of it—a $2,000 fine or even a $3,000 fine might look pretty good by comparison.

Still, word tends to get out when a company is one of the so-called free-riders—meaning it doesn't offer health coverage while so many other businesses do. It's not a good public relations move, and it certainly doesn't help the company compete for workers. About 95 percent of employers with more than fifty workers already offer health coverage, according to the Kaiser Family Foundation. So while there are sure to be some businesses that just send their employees to the new exchanges, there's not likely to be a mass move away from workplace coverage.

You Have Individual Health Insurance

The new rules for employers will have an impact on you only if you work at a business that doesn't offer health coverage. Some businesses might be more likely to offer you coverage—partly because of the new rules for employers, and partly because workers might demand that their employer offer health insurance so the workers don't get fined for being uninsured. On the other hand, some businesses will be less likely to offer it because their employees can just go to an exchange instead.

You're Uninsured

Again, the new expectations for employers will affect you only if you're uninsured because you work for a business that doesn't offer health coverage. You might get an offer of health coverage through the workplace. But the existence of health care exchanges, the new protections, and the expansion of Medicaid are likely to be bigger factors in whether you'll get health coverage. See Chapter 6 to read more about the exchanges, or Chapter 10 to learn about who will be eligible for the newly expanded Medicaid coverage.

You're on Medicare

The new rules for employers won't affect you.

You're on Medicaid

The new employer rules will affect you only if you work for a low-wage outfit—such as certain retail chains—that decides it's time to start offering health coverage.

You Have a Child in the State Children's Health Insurance Program

If you earn too much to get Medicaid coverage, even under the broader rules described in Chapter 10, it will be more important than ever to make sure your employer provides health coverage. That's because the State Children's Health Insurance Program has become vulnerable to state budget cuts as states struggle with the recession. In fact, Arizona has frozen enrollment in its program to save money, while two others—California and Tennessee—stopped enrolling new children for a while. If other states stop accepting new kids, you will be able to get coverage for your child in the new health care exchanges starting in 2014. But the benefits for children may not be as good as they are in the State Children's Health Insurance Program. See Chapter 10 for more details.

If your employer is open to adding health coverage, try to push for the best benefits for your children's needs that you can, because not all private insurance pays enough attention to their needs. Two groups that specialize in children's issues and are likely to have good advice on this are the Children's Defense Fund (1-800-CDF-1200 or www .childrensdefense.org) and First Focus (202-657-0670 or www.first focus.net).

You're an Early Retiree, Age Fifty-Five to Sixty-Four

Sad to say, you're in a different category from the rest of the people who get health benefits from an employer. The new law doesn't expect companies to offer retiree health coverage; it just gives them some financial help, until the health insurance exchanges begin, to make it a bit easier for them to cover your expenses. So if you get retiree health benefits from your former employer, there's a good chance that, in the long run, they'll drop your health benefits and let you get your coverage through a health insurance exchange.

For the short term, however, the new law has created a temporary "reinsurance" program to help companies cover the health costs of retirees. That means the federal government will basically insure the health insurance for some of your most expensive health care costs. Starting in June 2010 and ending when the insurance exchanges begin, in 2014, the program will pay for 80 percent of the costs between $15,000 and $90,000. It's possible that the program will end sooner if the money runs out. Still, it could keep your retiree health benefits going for a while.

By the time the exchanges are available, though, the incentives probably will change. The Employee Benefit Research Institute, a respected organization that studies health care and other benefits, predicts that employers will be less likely to offer retiree health benefits in the future. That's partly because, once the exchanges are available, there will be another place where you can get health coverage, and therefore less reason for your former employer to provide it. But it's also because the Medicare prescription drug benefit will get better, thanks to some changes described in Chapter 9 to close the gaps in coverage, and that will make it a better alternative to drug coverage through your former employer. And another change, described in Chapter 15, will start taxing the subsidies your former employer gets for giving you prescription drug coverage.

All of these changes may well make your former employer decide it's less important to provide retiree health benefits. But retiree health coverage has already been eroding for years, so unfortunately, this would not be a new trend. If the health insurance exchanges and the new insurance reforms work, together with the subsidies described in Chapter 4, it should become easier for you to get health coverage through other sources. But if it doesn't, it's important to let your senator or member of Congress know they need to make more changes to improve the new law.

6

The New Health
Insurance Exchanges

One of the biggest changes you'll see in the next few years is a new kind of forum, to be set up in every state, where you'll be able to get health coverage more easily than you could in the past. They will be a series of virtual marketplaces that offer a collection of health plans. The plans will all be under new rules and grouped together into categories, so people and small businesses can compare and apply for the one that fits their needs.

You'll deal with these exchanges mostly through their Web sites, which will let you compare health plans and apply online for the one you like best. Think of this as an Expedia for health care, and you'll get the idea. But the exchanges will do more than just provide information. They'll also set the rules for the health plans and put you into a larger "pool" of people so the cost of one illness doesn't triple the price of your coverage. These exchanges are the centerpiece of the new law's changes to private insurance, because the success of the reform's many moving parts—covering people with little or no health insurance, getting businesses to cover their workers, and giving people the protections they need—depends on how well the exchanges work.

In the past, if you didn't get your health insurance through the workplace or through a government program such as Medicare or Medicaid, you had just about no chance of getting good, stable health coverage. There were too many different kinds of health plans for individuals, lots of gaps in coverage, few rules, no good way to compare the plans and make an informed decision, and no way to spread your own health care costs among a broader group of people. Small businesses weren't able to do very well for themselves, either, largely because they couldn't spread their costs. Unless you were part of a large group, there wasn't much hope of making health insurance work for you.

The answer, smart people decided over the years, was to create a place where people and small businesses could become part of a larger group—and where there could be tighter rules so the health insurance plans didn't have as many ways to deny coverage to sick people. So the goals of the new health insurance exchanges are to give people a central place to shop for a health plan, set rules on what the plans have to cover and whom they have to accept, group all of the plans into a few standard categories based on how generous their coverage is, give everyone enough information so they can make an informed choice, and make it as easy as possible for people to apply.

There's already a real-world example of this: the Massachusetts health exchange, called Health Connector. Created under the state's 2006 health care reform law, it lets Massachusetts residents compare and apply for plans under set categories. They can get a gold, silver, or bronze plan, depending on how generous they want their coverage to be. There's also a young adult category, which has the narrowest benefits and the lowest premiums. Health Connector also helps people find out if they might be exempt from the rule that all state residents must get health insurance.

If you'd like to get a better idea of how a state health insurance exchange might work, take a look at the Massachusetts Health Connector Web site, which is the model for the exchanges that will be set up throughout the country. You can find it at www.mahealthconnector.org. Since the states will run their own exchanges, no two Web sites will look alike.

When President Obama was putting his health care proposal together for his presidential campaign, his advisers studied the Massachusetts system as a model for how a health insurance exchange could work. They decided to build his proposal around an exchange that would do the same kinds of things for the rest of the country. And while Congress made changes to his proposal, the law still keeps the exchange as a central focus of the big reforms. By 2019, as many as twenty-nine million Americans could be getting their health insurance through an exchange, according to the Congressional Budget Office, which tries to predict the impact of the bills Congress passes.

It will take a while to set up the exchanges. They're not supposed to begin until 2014, and that assumes the Department of Health and Human Services and the states can get all of the complicated preparation work done in time. There are still ways that people could get tripped up in shopping for health insurance, because the categories of health plans are broad enough that there can be a lot of important differences between the same kinds of plans. But if the exchanges work, they could make health insurance less of a nightmare than it was before.

Who's Eligible

The exchanges are intended for small businesses and for people who don't have another source of insurance. This means people who can't get health insurance through the workplace, aren't eligible for Medicare or Medicaid, aren't federal employees (who get health coverage through the Federal Employees Health Benefits Program), and aren't active military officers (who get coverage through TRICARE) or veterans (who get it through the Veterans Administration).

But there are exceptions. Remember that, as mentioned in Chapter 5, you can also go through the exchanges if the coverage offered by your employer is too expensive or doesn't cover enough of the health care costs. If you would have to pay more than 9.5 percent of your annual income for your employer's health coverage, or if the plan covers less than 60 percent of your costs, you can use your state's exchange instead. And if your employer's coverage would cost you between 8.0 and 9.5 percent of your annual income, you can get a tax-free voucher, worth the amount your employer would have paid toward your health insurance, and use it at the exchange instead.

Over time, the exchanges may become open to larger businesses as well. They're meant for businesses with one hundred workers or fewer, but starting in 2017, states will be able to open them up to companies with more than one hundred workers. And, yes, members of Congress and their staff will now have to go through the exchanges to get health insurance. They got tired of all the questions about whether they'd be willing to join the same health plans they were creating for the public.

How the Exchanges Work

The exchanges will be run by the states, under guidelines set by the Department of Health and Human Services. They will act like marketplaces where people can compare health plans on a Web site or get help with their research by calling a toll-free number. You would sign up using a standard enrollment form, either online or on paper. And when you join an individual or small business health plan, the exchanges have to add you to an insurance "pool" with other people in the same plan. This would likely make your premiums a lot more stable than in the current system, where one bad illness for you or a family member can send your premiums shooting into the stratosphere.

The exchanges will have a large role in setting the rules of the road for health insurers. They will certify insurers to offer their coverage (and kick them out if they break the rules), rate the plans, describe the different plans in a standard format that makes it easy to compare them, and allow people to use an online calculator to figure out how much they'd actually pay for a plan if they got the subsidies. Exchanges will also be the place where people can apply for an exemption from the requirement to get health insurance if it would be too much of a burden for them.

The states are supposed to run their own exchanges, but if they refuse to set one up, the Department of Health and Human Services has the authority to do it for them. The new law also requires that the states set up special exchanges for small businesses, called the Small Business Health Options Program, or SHOP. They can be either separate or part of the same exchange everyone else uses. One word of warning: Each exchange is supposed to be able to pay for itself starting in 2015, at which point it will be able to charge user fees.

The exchanges will not be the only way you will be able to get health insurance. Health insurance companies are allowed to offer plans outside the exchanges, and you will be able to look for coverage on your own if you want to. But the exchanges are likely to become the dominant place for most people to get their insurance, other than the workplace, since health insurance companies can get so much business by participating in them. And if you don't get coverage through the workplace, you're likely to find that your benefits and protections will be better—and your premiums will be more stable—if you get health insurance through an exchange rather than on your own.

What Kinds of Plans Will Be Available

The exchanges are supposed to offer health plans that will be lumped into categories so you can compare them easily. The categories will be labeled, similar to the way they do it in Massachusetts, so you can tell which plans are the most generous. Each label will tell you the "actuarial value"—the percent of covered benefits a plan is likely to pay—because you have to pay the rest. The more of the expenses you have to pay yourself, the cheaper the premiums will be.

Exchange Health Plans

Bronze:	60 percent coverage
Silver:	70 percent coverage
Gold:	80 percent coverage
Platinum:	90 percent coverage

By not listing the plans that limit their benefits too much, the exchanges can have an effect on the market by making it less profitable for insurance companies to offer such plans. But the exchanges can also offer catastrophic coverage, with lower premiums but more limited benefits, which are available only to people who are under thirty or who can't afford the other coverage. A "catastrophic" plan would cover at least three visits to your primary care doctor, but you'd have to pay out-of-pocket costs up to the same limits as for health savings accounts.

For 2010, those limits were $5,950 a year for individual coverage and $11,900 a year for family coverage.

The only problem with the way the law designs the categories is that "actuarial value" can be misleading if you don't know exactly what it means. Congress picked it as an easy way to measure how much coverage a health plan actually provides. The problem is that you might think a plan that offers, say, 80 percent coverage will cover exactly 80 percent of your personal costs. In reality, that's just the average for what the plan will cover for an average group of people, with the normal mix of healthy and sick people. For you personally, it will pay a different share. And if you're reasonably healthy, it's likely to be a lot less than 80 percent.

Here's why: If you're like most people, who don't use the health care system all that much, your medical costs in any given year may not be that much higher than your deductible, which is the amount you have to pay before your plan starts sharing the costs. If you have a deductible of, say, $1,000, and your medical expenses for the year are $1,200, then your plan won't come close to paying 80 percent of your health care costs. It will pay 80 percent only as an average spread across a large group of people, which will include a few people with expensive illnesses and a majority who don't get sick very much. So you can still use the categories to get a rough sense of how much the plans cover, but don't be fooled into thinking that they tell you exactly what you'll pay each year.

There's also a lot of room to design the benefits differently in each category. We've learned that through the example of the Medicare Advantage program, which contracts with private insurers to provide Medicare benefits. Medicare Advantage plans are also measured by "actuarial value." But according to the Center on Budget and Policy Priorities—a think tank that studies how policies affect low-income people—some plans have been able to design their benefits to gently steer away the people with the most health problems. For example, such plans will cover less of the costs for a hospital stay than Medicare usually pays, but more of the costs of a gym membership. As long as the total coverage adds up to the same "actuarial value" of benefits, they're allowed to do that.

It should help that the new law defines a lot of the benefits that have to be included in the exchange plans, and the Department of Health and Human Services is supposed to put out more detailed guidelines based on what's included in a typical employer health plan. But when you search for plans, it's a good idea to look for clues that one of them might be trying to avoid sick people. If you see a lot of frills but unusually strict limits on what the plan will pay for hospital costs—or anything else you might need if you get seriously sick—stay away from that plan. There might be another one in the same category, at about the same price, that would give you better protection in case you don't stay healthy forever.

What Kind of Information You'll Get

The information you'll see when shopping for health plans should be a good deal better than it is now. Besides the standard format for describing the plans, the ratings of the plans, and the cost-sharing calculator, you will see summaries of the health plans that will be improved by new rules that should kick in no later than 2011. For the first time, health plans will have to give you a Web address where you can look at the actual certificate of coverage—the line-by-line description of everything the plan does and does not cover. They'll also have to describe what they don't cover in their more general plan description. And, also for the first time, they'll have to describe what you might pay in a typical high-cost situation, such as a pregnancy or a serious illness.

Once the exchanges are up and running, you'll also be able to look up what kind of cost-sharing you might pay for a particular medical service—including the deductible, copayments, and coinsurance. You'll also have access to a lot of other information on the plan, including its payment policies, how many people are enrolled in it, how many have left the plan, the number of claims it has denied, how it rates people to determine their premiums, and what kind of cost-sharing it requires when you go out of its network of doctors and hospitals.

What Kind of Help You'll Get

The states and the exchanges are supposed to set up ombudsman offices to help you with the kinds of issues you might run into. They're supposed to help you enroll in plans, help you file complaints and appeals, help you if you're having trouble getting the premium tax credit, track the kinds of problems you and other people are having with the health plans, and educate you about your rights and responsibilities. There's $30 million in federal funding available to help the states set up these ombudsman offices.

Another feature that the exchanges will offer will be a "navigator" program, which will give grants to outside groups to spread the word about the health plans and tax credits that are available. They're supposed to give impartial information about the plans, help people enroll, and put them in touch with an ombudsman if they're having trouble. A "navigator" could be a trade association, a nonprofit, a chamber of commerce, a union, a ranching or farming organization, or a small business development center. It cannot be a health insurance company, though. The exchanges are supposed to make sure there won't be any conflict of interest.

Abortion

You may have heard that there was a fight over abortion coverage while Congress was working on this bill. The issue was whether people who go through the exchanges for health insurance, and use the tax credit to do so, should be able to use that federal subsidy to pay for a plan that covers abortions. It wasn't about the millions of Americans who will get their health coverage outside the exchanges, and it wasn't about the five million Americans who are likely to use the exchanges but who won't need the tax credit.

But with twenty-four million other Americans expected to use the exchanges, this was a big enough group of people to bring back one of the oldest fights in the culture wars. For more than three decades, there has been a ban on using federal Medicaid funds to pay for abortions except in cases of rape, incest, or danger to the mother's life. For anti-abortion Democrats, there was no reason federal taxpayers should have to start paying for abortions. For Democrats who support abortion rights, however, people in the exchanges would also use their own money, so any restrictions on abortion coverage would mean that they couldn't use their own money to get coverage for a legal procedure.

But Democrats couldn't get the health care bill through the House without the support of antiabortion Democrats such as Bart Stupak of Michigan, and they couldn't get it through the Senate without satisfying Democrat Ben Nelson of Nebraska, who refused to vote for the bill unless it had a strong firewall to keep federal money from being used for abortions. Without Nelson, the Democrats wouldn't have had the sixty votes that allowed them to pass the health care bill in the Senate. And, if anything, Stupak and his House allies wanted a stronger firewall than Nelson did.

The solution the Democrats came up with was to let states pass laws to ban abortion coverage in the exchange plans. And under the new law, any plan that offers abortion coverage has to keep the federal subsidy funds separate so they aren't used to pay for abortion. So if you wanted to buy a health plan that covered abortion, you would have to write two checks, one for the abortion coverage and one for everything else. To convince Stupak and his allies that this was really enough to prevent federal funding of abortion, Obama also issued an executive order confirming that the money can't be used for abortions and telling the Department of Health and Human Services to give states guidance on how to make sure the money is kept separate.

It may be a while before we know the practical impact of this abortion compromise, but it's already clear that it didn't really satisfy anybody. Groups that support abortion rights say it will discourage insurance companies from covering abortions, so as a practical reality, the procedure will become less and less available. But the antiabortion side says the law still wouldn't keep other people's federal funds from indirectly paying for abortion coverage, because it's too easy to mix the money. And they don't think Obama's executive order does anything except restate the law.

It was a serious issue, and the people who care about it care deeply. But it's also important to keep it in perspective. If it affects you, it affects you deeply and profoundly. But for everyone else, there are many other parts of the law that will affect you far more on a daily basis.

Illegal Immigrants

Another political fight that Congress had to settle was over how tough the new law should be on illegal immigrants. The House wanted to ban them from getting the tax credit to help them buy a health plan through the exchanges, but not from buying a health insurance exchange plan if they paid for it themselves. The Senate wanted to ban illegal immigrants from buying any health plan through the exchanges under any circumstances—either with subsidies or their own money.

In the end, the Senate won. To participate at all in the exchanges, people have to be in the country legally and be able to prove it. Anyone else will be unable to buy coverage, even with their own money. Some House Democrats argued that this was unfair, since it would mean that anyone who wasn't here legally would have to get their health care in emergency rooms—and the cost probably would get passed on to the rest of us. In the end, this argument didn't threaten the passage of the bill. But there probably will be future debates about what is the right way to provide health care to illegal immigrants.

What Massachusetts Learned from Their System

On the surface, the Massachusetts health care reform, which was similar to what the new federal law is trying to do, was a big success. By 2008, more than 97 percent of the state's residents had some form of health coverage, which is as close to universal coverage as any state in the country. But a study by the Henry J. Kaiser Family Foundation found that a lot of Massachusetts residents still find health care too expensive, including low-income people who can get coverage through the workplace and middle-income people who don't have workplace coverage. Neither group can get subsidies for their health coverage, so they still go without medical care because they don't think they can afford it.

The lesson is that even when lawmakers try to reform the health care system, they can't cover all of people's costs. And expenses that they think should be affordable—such as costs under $1,000—really aren't affordable for most people. So it will be important not to expect the new health insurance exchanges to solve all of the problems of the health care system. But federal and state health care officials need to know what's not working so they can keep track of what else about the law needs to be changed. So when you run into problems, let the ombudsman know. Let your congressman or senator know, too.

Change	Effective Date
Health insurance exchanges	January 1, 2014

What Do You Do If . . .

You Work for a Small Business

If you already have insurance through the workplace, it might change, but not until 2014. Once the exchanges are available, your employer might decide to switch to a small group plan that has a larger insurance "pool." This can help them spread health costs among more people and make their premiums more stable. The standards for those plans might help your employer find one that doesn't have big gaps in coverage, too. For example, starting in 2014, small group health plans can't have deductibles higher than $2,000 for individuals and $4,000 for families. Those limits will increase over the years by an amount that's tied to the growth in premiums.

If your business doesn't offer you insurance yet, now is a good time to get on their case. The first open enrollment period will be announced by the Department of Health and Human Services no later than July 2012, and there will be annual open enrollment periods every year after that.

You Work for a Medium-Size or Large Company

You probably won't ever deal with an exchange, unless your state opens it up to businesses with more than one hundred workers. The first year it can do that is 2017. But if you can't get health insurance through your workplace, or the only coverage you can get there is too expensive, the exchange will be an option for you. You should be able to figure out if you qualify by using the exchange's online calculator, which is supposed to help you predict the cost of coverage, including after any subsidies you might receive.

A quick reminder: If the only health insurance available would cost more than 9.5 percent of your annual income, or cover less than 60 percent of the costs, you can get a subsidy and go to your state's exchange. And if it would cost between 8.0 and 9.5 percent of your annual income to buy coverage, you can get a voucher from your employer and use it at the exchange. See Chapter 5 for more information.

You Have Individual Health Insurance

You can keep what you have if you're happy with it, and you may still be able to get individual insurance outside of the exchange. But the exchange is likely to become the most common way for people to get health insurance on their own, and the insurance industry will probably reshape its products to fit that new market. If nothing else, the ability to get yourself into an insurance "pool" with other people should make your own costs more predictable than they have been with your old insurance.

If you're interested in switching to a new individual insurance plan through an exchange, the first open enrollment period will be announced by the Department of Health and Human Services no later than July 2012, and there will be annual open enrollment periods every year.

You're Uninsured

Watch for the first open enrollment period for the new exchange, which should be announced by the Department of Health and Human Services no later than July 2012. Then there will be regular open enrollment periods every year. If your main concern about health insurance is the price, the calculator on the exchange's Web site should be able to help you figure out what you're likely to pay and which plan you might be able to afford. It's supposed to help you factor in the tax credit subsidy you can get. If you want an idea of how this online calcu-lator might work, there is already a pretty good one available at the Web site of the Henry J. Kaiser Family Foundation (www.kff.org).

Another change that should help make health insurance more stable is that states will charge fees to plans with healthier-than-average people and give the money to plans that have people with more health risks. That way, some plans can't make as much money by attracting all the healthy people, leaving sicker patients behind in other plans to face ever-rising premiums.

You're on Medicare

The exchanges won't affect you, because they are meant to help people get private insurance.

You're on Medicaid

The exchanges won't affect you if you're already enrolled. However, if you're applying for health coverage for the first time through an ex-change, there is supposed to be a process that determines whether you're eligible for Medicaid. If you are, it will enroll you automatically. This process will have to be designed by the Department of Health and Human Services before the exchanges begin.

You Have a Child in the State Children's Health Insurance Program

The exchanges won't affect you if your child is already enrolled. How-ever, if you're applying for health coverage for the first time through an exchange, there is supposed to be a process that determines whether your child is eligible for the State Children's Health Insurance Pro-gram. If your child is, it will enroll the child automatically. This process will have to be designed by the Department of Health and Human Services before the exchanges begin.

You're an Early Retiree, Age Fifty-Five to Sixty-Four

As discussed in Chapter 5, your employer may be less tempted to offer you retiree health insurance benefits once the exchanges are available. So an exchange may become your best hope of getting and keeping health coverage. The first open enrollment period should be announced by the Department of Health and Human Services no later than July 2012.

Because you'll be "pooled" with other people to spread everyone's health costs among a larger group, your state's exchange should help you get cheaper coverage than you could have gotten on your own before. It should also help that states are supposed to prevent insurers from "cherry-picking" people, luring away the healthiest people, while everyone with health problems gets lumped into a few plans with sky-high premiums. The states are supposed to prevent this by charging fees to plans with healthier-than-average people and giving the money to plans that have people with more health risks.

Still, there's no guarantee that health coverage through an exchange will be cheaper than the retiree benefits you had through your former employer. If they're not, you should let the state ombudsman know, because your exchange might need to recruit a different set of plans or monitor its current plans more closely. There may also be a way to report problems through the Department of Health and Human Services Web site (www.hhs.gov).

Finally, you should let your senator or congressman know if your situation has become worse under the new law. The official Senate and House Web sites (www.senate.gov and www.house.gov) or privately run Web sites such as Congress.org (www.congress.org) and Project Vote Smart (www.votesmart.org) are all good resources.

7

What's Left of the Public Option?

Nothing captured the deep split over the role of government in our health care system better than the fight over the "public option." It was supposed to be one of the choices available in the exchanges—a health care plan run by the government instead of private insurers, a kind of mini-Medicare for people who wanted to get health insurance on their own. Conservatives fretted that it would become a slippery slope leading to government-run health care for everybody, while liberals were thrilled at the idea that they might have a choice other than private insurance companies, whom they didn't trust. The whole thing got blown way out of proportion. In the end, it was the moderate Democrats who shot it down—and all that's left in the new law is a shell of the original idea.

The point of the public option was to give some competition to the private insurance companies, forcing them to become more efficient, bring down their costs, and provide better care. The idea started as an expansion of the actual Medicare program, an approach that political scientist Jacob Hacker proposed in 2003. His idea, called Medicare

Plus, was to put everyone who wasn't already in Medicare or a work-place health plan into a broader Medicare program. That way, people on Medicaid or other public programs could all be in one group, rather than in a crazy patchwork of different programs, and uninsured people could buy into it as well. There wouldn't have been any threat to people who like their private insurance, Hacker said, because they could have stayed in it. But everyone who was falling through the cracks would have had somewhere to go.

The idea quickly caught on with liberals, who saw it as a way to escape from what they didn't like about private health insurance—the constant rejections and hassles, the gaps in coverage, and decisions that always seemed to be driven by profits. By 2007, when Barack Obama began his campaign for the presidency, the idea had morphed into a "public option" that would put health insurance companies in their place. Obama certainly talked about the public option during the campaign, but only as one of many pieces that had to fit together to make health care reform work. By the time he took office, however, it had become the one piece of health care reform that liberals had to have—and the piece that conservatives and moderates used to scare people about the government taking over their health care.

When Republicans griped during the health care debate that liberals really wanted the public option to turn into a "single-payer" system—the kind Canada uses, where the government pays for everyone's medical care—they weren't completely off. A lot of Democrats did want a single-payer system, and saw the public option as the next best thing. Some House Democrats insisted they had already compromised by agreeing not to fight for a single-payer system. John Edwards—remember him?—put in a strong pitch for the public option when he ran against Obama for the Democratic presidential nomination, and he often suggested that if people really liked the public option, it might lead to a single-payer system someday.

Obama never saw it that way. He insisted that the competition with private insurance companies was a good enough reason to include the public option. Because a government-run health plan would have more limited overhead costs and wouldn't have to worry about keeping profits high, he argued, it could give private insurance companies a reason to keep their worst practices in check. But as we now know, he was never as enthusiastic about it as a lot of liberals in the Democratic Party. If there were another way to compete with private insurers and give them a reason to bring their costs down, Obama often said, that would be okay, too.

What most people never realized about the public option was how limited it would have been. It was only for people who would have had to go through an exchange to get their health insurance. People who had health coverage through the workplace could not have joined the public option, even if they wanted to. At most, about four million Americans might have signed up for it, according to the Congressional Budget Office—only about one out of every seven people who got their health coverage through an exchange.

But the big fight was about the wisdom of creating a new public plan at all. For Republicans, it became Exhibit A that the Democrats actually wanted government-run health care for everyone. And the very idea of government-run health care scared enough moderate Democrats in the Senate—including Joe Lieberman of Connecticut, an independent who sides with the Democrats—that the party couldn't round up enough votes to get the health care bill through the Senate. Lieberman, in particular, insisted he would never vote for a government-run option of any kind. So Senate Democrats had to find an alternative that might satisfy some of the original goals of the public option, but that wouldn't scare away the votes they needed.

Multistate Plans

Their answer was to allow private health insurers to create national plans—but plans that would be supervised by a federal agency. Once the new health exchanges are open, the U.S. Office of Personnel Management, which runs the health plans for members of Congress, would contract with private insurers to offer at least two health plans that would be available in every state. One of the plans would have to be a nonprofit.

This would be a way of splitting the difference between public and private health coverage. The Office of Personnel Management would negotiate the contracts for the health plans, just as it does for the health plans for members of Congress. It would bargain with the plans to determine what premiums they would charge, how much of the premiums they would have to spend on medical care, and how much of a profit they could make. But the actual health plans would be run by private insurers and nonprofits, not the federal government.

The U.S. Office of Personnel Management will have to have at least two national private plans ready to offer through the health insurance exchanges by January 1, 2014. They will have to offer all of the benefits that are required in the other exchange plans, and they will have to meet all of the minimum standards of the health care program for federal workers.

This would be a way of trying to re-create the success of the Federal Employees Health Benefits Program, the health program for members of Congress and federal workers. It's a menu of health plans that provides plenty of choices to everyone in the program, including a Blue

Cross Blue Shield plan. Most of the coverage is fairly generous, and because the plans have plenty of federal employees to spread the costs, it is more affordable than it would be for smaller groups. Democrats have often proposed that people should have a way to get health coverage as good as that enjoyed by members of Congress.

Unfortunately, there are a lot of unknowns about the multistate plans, and they probably won't create the same level of competition many people hoped the public option would have provided. The Congressional Budget Office didn't think the plans would do much to force premiums down in the other plans in the health insurance exchanges—unlike the public option, which it thought would have reduced premiums more. The budget office said there was no guarantee that private insurers would be interested in creating a national plan, and it raised doubts that nonprofits alone could do the job.

And although the Office of Personnel Management has plenty of bargaining power with its health plans, even the Federal Employees Health Benefits Program has had some pretty steep premium hikes lately. In 2010, for example, the average premiums went up 8.8 percent. So it's not clear that the multistate plans would do any better at holding costs down. They may give you more health insurance choices, which could be an improvement in itself—especially if you'd rather get your coverage from a nonprofit than a for-profit insurance company. But don't expect them to give you big savings on your health care premiums.

Co-ops

There is also another alternative in the new law: health care cooperatives. The law sets aside $6 billion in federal funds to help set up nonprofit health insurance plans to be run by consumers. Under the Consumer Operated and Oriented Plan (CO-OP), you might have another nonprofit option in your state if you'd rather not get your health care from a for-profit insurance company. But this will happen only if enough cooperatives are launched, with enough strength to provide a real challenge to the insurance companies, and that's not certain at all.

The idea came from yet another attempt to find a compromise for senators who didn't like the public option. Senator Kent Conrad, a moderate Democrat from North Dakota, thought about his state's experiences with co-ops and decided it might be a good model to try with health care. This way, private insurers would have competition, but the co-ops would be run by consumers, not the federal government.

You might think of co-ops as being more successful in other industries, such as agriculture. (Think of Land O'Lakes, which is a co-op.) But there is also a very successful health care co-op in the Seattle area, Group Health Cooperative of Puget Sound, which is highly regarded and drew attention during the health care debate as a possible model for reform. Its members elect an eleven-member board of trustees and vote on the bylaws of the organization, and the board makes the policy decisions and hires the top leaders.

The problem is that co-ops are extremely hard to set up, especially with so many established insurance plans dominating the market. Group Health Cooperative has been around since 1947, so it's not new to the market. It's also the only one that has survived from the 1930s and 1940s, the height of the cooperative movement. All of the rest died out, because they were small and didn't have enough resources. When the Congressional Budget Office studied the proposed co-op program in the new law, it concluded that co-ops "seem unlikely to establish a significant market presence in many areas of the country."

So, if you see one in your area in the next few years, it may be one more option that might be managed better than private insurance companies. But don't count on it. It may be years before the co-ops even get going—if they get going at all.

Other Health Plans in More Than One State

Another option in the new law would allow health insurers to sell the same health plan in different states, but only under a fairly strict set of rules. Starting in 2016, the states could join a new kind of agreement called Health Care Choice Compacts, which would allow insurance companies to sell individual insurance in two or more states as long as they obey the consumer protection laws in those states. They might not have to cover all of the benefits your state requires, but they would at least have to cover all of the minimum benefits that have to be offered in health insurance exchanges. (See Chapter 2.)

This option grew out of a long-running dispute between Republicans and Democrats about how to make cheaper health plans available. Many Republicans have suggested letting insurance companies sell health plans across state lines. The idea is that if you live in a state that makes health insurance too expensive, because it requires the plans to cover too many things, you should be able to buy a plan from another state that doesn't make it so expensive. Even though every benefit mandated by a state might seem like a good idea, the argument goes, the mandates add up—and the cost puts health insurance out of reach for many people.

The problem with that idea, Democrats say, is that if you don't set at least some basic rules for these plans, every health insurance company will set up their headquarters in a state with practically no rules at all. And then they will be free to sell lousy insurance to unsuspecting customers. That's called a "race to the bottom." So the Democrats were only willing to allow health insurance companies to sell across state lines if there were some basic rules attached.

For one thing, the health plans can't undermine the new health exchanges by offering fewer benefits. They have to at least follow the exchange rules—although those rules may still allow the plans to be less expensive than they would be in some states. And they will have to comply with each state's consumer protection laws, restrictions on how they can sell their products, and rules on how to avoid unfair trade practices.

It's not clear that these health plans would save you that much money when you factor in all of these rules—if insurers even bother to offer them. But if they don't make a big difference in the price, that will prove that the only way to bring prices down in a big way is to get rid of benefits and consumer protection rules that many people consider important.

Health Plan	Effective Date
Multistate Plans	January 1, 2014
Co-ops	July 1, 2013 (deadline to award federal startup loans and grants)
Health Care Choice Compacts	January 1, 2016

8

While You're Waiting . . .

So Congress has passed the health care bill, President Obama has signed it into law, and everyone has spent an awful lot of time congratulating themselves. The political fight goes on—the tea partiers are furious, and Republicans are campaigning on repealing the law. But otherwise, it's over. The law is on the books, the press conferences have trailed off, and the cable news networks have moved on to the latest celebrity and/or crime story that doesn't really matter. So you're probably asking the natural question: "Is it fixed yet?"

Unfortunately, the answer is no. The biggest health care changes will take a while to set up, so they won't kick in until 2014. The health insurance exchanges, the tax credits to help you get insurance, the new benefits package, the ban on turning you down because of preexisting conditions, the rules against charging you more because of health problems—all of these are still a few years off in the future. For Obama and the Democrats in Congress, that's a problem. After all, 2014 isn't just one election away. It's *two* elections away—including the one where Obama will be up for reelection.

That's why the authors of the law threw in a package of quick changes so people will be satisfied that something is happening. Some of the changes are permanent; others are only temporary. But they're all designed to give people at least some relief from the problems of the old system. Think of them as a down payment on the changes still to come. And if they create problems, there might be time for federal and state health officials to learn from them and tweak some of the plans for the bigger reforms.

The First Changes You'll See

Here are the early changes that will affect you most directly:

No Lifetime Limits, and Stricter Rules on Annual Limits

Although this will affect only a small number of people, if you have an expensive health condition and need ongoing care, you will be able to keep getting that care without worrying that your coverage will run out. Right now it's common for health insurance policies to limit what they'll pay for over your lifetime, sometimes capping your benefits at $1 million to $2 million. That practice will have to end for all private health insurance plans, including the ones that are in effect right now, in September 2010.

Another change: The Department of Health and Human Services will put tighter rules on how much workplace health plans and new individual insurance plans can limit your benefits every year. By 2014, insurers won't be able to cap your annual benefits at all.

Coverage Not Cancelled for People Who Get Sick

This practice, called "rescissions," is basically an insurance company's way of finding an excuse to drop you if you're going to cost them money. Starting in September 2010, they won't be able to do that any-more. This is mainly an issue for the individual health insurance market. If you're in a group health plan, such as your employer's health insurance, they don't do this.

Children No Longer Turned Down for Preexisting Conditions

This won't be true for grown-ups until 2014, but for now, you can take some comfort in knowing that if you have kids, they'll be able to get health insurance. That means common conditions such as asthma won't keep them from being covered anymore. If you're getting health insurance through the workplace, or if you apply for individual health insurance starting in September 2010, your children will be protected.

Temporary Risk Pools Set Up

Since not all of the new protections that would help you get health insurance will be in place right away, the new law requires that the Department of Health and Human Services set up a temporary "high-risk pool" program to be available in every state. This will be a place you can go to get health coverage on your own if you have a preexisting condition and private insurers are turning you down. Thirty-four states already have them, but they will have to operate under rules set up by the new law. For example, they will have to cover 65 percent of your costs, and they can vary your premiums only by the size of your family, where you live, and your age. (Older people can still be charged four times as much as everybody else in the risk pools, which is more variation than you would have in the exchange health plans that start in 2014.)

By the time this book comes out, if all goes smoothly, the high-risk pool program should be up and running. It's supposed to be available starting in July 2010. However, it is possible that the Department of Health and Human Services will not have enough time to set this up throughout the country by the deadline. As this book went to press, HHS was negotiating with the states to find out how many of them were willing to set up these risk pools on their own. The states that already have them may have to create new ones that meet all of the new rules, and the ones that don't can either create them or contract with a private carrier to do so. If they don't set up any program at all, Health and Human Services will have to create a multistate program for them, without much time to get it going. This temporary program will end when the health insurance exchanges are available, in 2014.

Young Adults Stay on Their Parents' Plans

Since young adults under thirty make up about a third of the uninsured, this will be an important element in trying to bring them into the system. Beginning in September 2010, anyone under age twenty-six will be allowed to stay on their parents' health care plan as a dependent (which includes all health plans that are in effect now). This is similar to laws already in place in twenty-five states, which allow young adults to stay on their parents' plan into their mid-twenties.

This is a solution that won't work in all cases. It works only if the parents have coverage, it's not available to young adults who could get their own coverage through the workplace, and some employers charge a lot more for dependent coverage. But it's one more step that might make it easier for some twentysomethings to get health insurance.

Small Business Tax Credit Established

The first phase of the tax credit starts in 2010. Small businesses with up to twenty-five employees and average wages of up to $50,000 will be able to get a credit for up to 35 percent of their premium expenses, depending on their size and how much their workers are paid. This will be available until 2014, when the credit will increase to 50 percent.

From then on, though, small businesses will be able to get it for only two years. See Chapter 4 for more details.

Preventive Services Covered

If you join a new private health plan after September 2010, you will have full coverage of the preventive services that are recommended by official government advisory panels, such as screenings for various diseases and annual flu shots. And state Medicaid programs will have to cover antismoking programs for pregnant women starting in October 2010. See Chapter 12 for more details.

Better Information Available on Plan Options

By the time this book comes out, the Department of Health and Human Services should have a new Web portal that will tell you what kinds of coverage might be available to you through private insurance, Medicaid, the State Children's Health Insurance Program, or high-risk pools for people who can't get private health insurance because of medical problems. It probably will be linked to the official Department of Health and Human Services Web site, so check www.hhs.gov for the latest.

The site won't have the kind of detail you're likely to find once the health insurance exchanges are available, because it's not possible to build that kind of site that quickly. But for now, it is supposed to let you know what you're eligible for, what the premiums might be, how much you might have to pay in cost-sharing, and what's available in each health plan. It won't list limited-benefit plans, a step that's intended to steer as many consumers away from them as possible.

Over time, the information available should start to improve. By the end of March 2011—a year after Obama signed the health care reforms into law—there should be new standards requiring the plans to come up with better, easier-to-understand descriptions. They'll have to list the benefits, what's not covered, how much of the costs the health plan will pay, and what expenses you'd have to pay. They'll also have to describe what you might have to pay if you or a family member has a certain kind of serious illness, and they'll have to direct you to a Web site where you can look at the plan's "evidence of coverage" document, with the fine points of what is and isn't covered. Health insurers will have to start using these descriptions by the end of March 2012.

Better Appeal Rights

Beginning in September 2010, all new private health plans will have to give you two levels of appeals if they have refused to pay for a medical service. You'll be able to appeal directly to the plan—something that's called an "internal appeal," which is already available now to most people. But you also will have the right to file an "external appeal," where you take your case to independent medical reviewers. As discussed in Chapter 1, that's available in only eighteen states now.

Help with Health Care Costs for Early Retirees

Since people between the ages of fifty-five and sixty-four often have significant health care costs, there will be a temporary program to provide "reinsurance" to help employers cover these costs. The program starts in June 2010, and it's basically a way to pay some of the costs so the employers can, in theory, pass on some of the savings to the retirees by lowering their premiums. It will cover 80 percent of the costs, and it's good for any expenses between $15,000 and $90,000. The help is available only until the money runs out, though. With $5 billion to spend between now and 2014, the program could easily get to the point where they have to stop taking applications.

More of Premiums Spent on Health Care

Starting in 2011, health plans will have to start refunding some of your premium payments if they're keeping too much of it for profits or spending it on administrative costs. If it's a group plan and it spends less than 85 percent of your premiums on health care, or it's a small group or individual insurance plan and it spends less than 80 percent of your premiums on health care, you have to get a refund once a year.

Premium Hikes Discouraged

Between now and 2014, health insurance companies will have to justify any premium increases to the Department of Health and Human Services and state insurance agencies. They'll also have to post notices of the increases on their Web sites. That's a way of trying to discourage health insurers from going overboard with premium hikes before the health insurance exchanges are available. If any insurer boosts premiums too much, state insurance commissioners can recommend that they be locked out of the exchanges.

Money for Ombudsman Offices

There is extra money in the new law to help states beef up their ombudsman and consumer assistance offices, which will be your first stop in most cases when you're having trouble with your health plan. These offices will be expected to help you file complaints and appeals, keep track of the kinds of problems consumers are having, teach you about your rights, and help you sign up for coverage. And when the exchanges begin in 2014, they're supposed to help you if you're having trouble getting the tax credits to help pay your premiums.

There will be $30 million in federal funds to divide up among the states. Unfortunately, some states have better consumer offices than others, and the new law probably won't change that. But the extra funds should at least help many of the offices deal with their new responsibilities.

"Donut Hole" for Medicare Prescription Drug Coverage Begins to Close

The infamous "donut hole" in Medicare prescription drug coverage is the gap where Medicare stops covering your drug expenses for a while and doesn't start again until your bills have gotten a lot higher. Starting in 2010, the new law will start to phase out that gap. You'll get a $250 rebate in 2010, and the gap is supposed to close gradually over time, until it's gone completely by 2020. See Chapter 9 for more information.

Change	Effective Date
Financial help for early retirees	June 2010
Temporary risk pool	July 2010
Health and Human Services Web site established for coverage options	July 2010
No lifetime coverage limits	September 23, 2010
Restrictions on annual limits	September 23, 2010
Coverage no longer cancelled for sick people	September 23, 2010
Children no longer turned down for preexisting conditions	September 23, 2010
Young adults under twenty-six can stay on their parents' health care plans	September 23, 2010
Better appeal rights	September 23, 2010
Preventive services covered	September 23, 2010
Small business tax credit available	First phase starts in 2010

Medicare "donut hole" closing*	Starts in 2010
Unreasonable premium increases monitored	2010
Money for ombudsman offices available	2010
Better health plan descriptions available	Standards must be issued in 2011; health plans have to comply by 2012
Health plan profits limited	2011

What Do You Do If . . .

You Work for a Small Business

You should encourage your employer to take advantage of the first phase of tax credits, which may help them provide you with health coverage if they don't already. You will also get the benefit of many of the early changes, including the ban on lifetime coverage limits, the ability to keep your child on your plan until age twenty-six, the preventive services, the better appeal rights, the improved descriptions of the coverage, and the limits on profits.

You Work for a Medium-Size or Large Company

A lot of these early changes are aimed at people trying to get health insurance on their own, so they may not be that useful to you. Some could be helpful to you, such as the ban on lifetime coverage limits and the ability to keep your child on your plan until age twenty-six. The

---

*It won't be completely closed until 2020.

same goes for the new appeal rights, although you may have a lot of these already.

You Have Individual Health Insurance

Some of the immediate changes should apply to you in your current health plan, including the elimination of lifetime limits and the ban on dropping you if you get sick. Others, however, apply only to new individual insurance plans. These include the requirement to cover your child's preexisting conditions, the restrictions on annual coverage limits, the coverage of preventive services, and the better appeal rights.

There seems to be some confusion about whether you get this last set of protections if you have individual health insurance right now. In researching this book, I got conflicting answers from government officials on whether you would automatically get these protections, or whether you would have to switch to a new plan to be sure. This may be clarified once the official Department of Health and Human Services rules come out. If you want to be sure, though, check with your health plan to see if you're going to get these protections starting in September 2010. If not, or if you don't get a clear answer, you may need to switch to a new plan.

If you're interested in switching, it's a good idea to look at the new Department of Health and Human Services Web site, which should go live in July 2010. It should be able to help you compare a lot of different options with more information than is available now. And if you're in a limited-benefit plan now, the Web site might help you find something that would give you more protection than you have now. If you don't want to wait until then, or if the HHS Web site is delayed, you can still compare your options fairly well through private Web sites such as eHealthInsurance.com.

However, another good reason to wait is that most of the new protections don't kick in until September 2010. When you are ready to look for a new plan, study the plan description carefully to make sure it does, in fact, comply with the new rules. If you don't see signs that the insurer has adapted to the changes, it would be a good idea to look at other plans or wait a little bit longer.

You're Uninsured

Most of the early changes are aimed at you. They won't make health insurance any cheaper, unfortunately. The changes that will, if they work, are still a few years off. But if you are uninsured now because you haven't been able to get coverage, it might help to get into a temporary high-risk pool. These will be available to anyone with a preexisting condition, so they'll at least give you somewhere to go, especially since sixteen states and the District of Columbia don't have their own risk pools yet.

The only thing to be careful of, though, is that state risk pools haven't always been a great option. A lot of them charge expensive premiums because everyone in them has a health problem, and in some states they've had to cut off enrollment because they don't have the funding for more people. The new rules could make some of the risk pools better, but they might still have to cut off enrollment at some point, since there's only a fixed amount of money—$5 billion—available. If you do join a risk pool, the Department of Health and Human Services is supposed to come up with a smooth way to move you into a health insurance exchange plan when they are ready in 2014.

If you have kids, you may also be able to get them insured more easily, since health insurance companies won't be able to reject them for preexisting conditions anymore. And you'll be able to get health insurance that doesn't limit what it will cover over your lifetime, or annually. The new Department of Health and Human Services Web site should make comparison shopping a little bit easier, and by the end of September the new rules should take effect.

Check the plan descriptions, though, to make sure they reflect the new rules. If they don't, you might want to keep looking, or wait a bit longer until all of the health plans have adapted. The HHS Web site should also be able to tell you if your income is low enough for you to qualify for Medicaid or the State Children's Health Insurance Program.

You're on Medicare

You should see changes beginning in 2010 as they start to close the "donut hole" in your prescription drug coverage. In practical terms, though, the savings might be less than you'd expect. For one thing, the "hole" is supposed to be only $250 smaller in 2010 than it would have been otherwise. And remember that until the gap is completely gone, in 2020, there will still be a range of drug costs that you'll have to pay yourself. For 2010, you might have to pay all of the drug costs starting when you've had $2,830 in drug expenses, and ending when you've had $6,440 in expenses—a $3,610 gap in coverage. And since the gap was expected to grow pretty fast under the old law, it might be a few years before the new coverage catches up and actually makes it shrink. See Chapter 9 for more information.

You're on Medicaid

Most of the policy changes don't affect you if you're already in the program. The main one that might help you is the new coverage of services to help pregnant women stop smoking. But the new Department of Health and Human Services Web site might make it easier for you to find out if you are eligible for Medicaid.

You Have a Child in the State Children's Health Insurance Program

The policy changes won't affect you if you already have a child in the program. If you don't, the new Department of Health and Human Services Web site might make it easier for you to find out if your child is eligible.

You're an Early Retiree, Age Fifty-Five to Sixty-Four

If you get retiree health benefits, you might get some short-term relief from the "reinsurance" program to help your former employer pay some of your biggest health care expenses. You should think of it as only short-term relief, though, as the program will be around only until the exchanges begin or the money runs out. And even though there might be a push in Congress to provide more funding after it runs out, there's no way of knowing who will be in charge then. Critics of organized labor already are chipping away at the program, charging that it's mainly a giveaway to unions. (The law doesn't make any distinction between union members and non-union members, but retiree health benefits are most commonly offered by large companies with unions.)

If you don't have retiree health benefits and you're searching for health coverage, the temporary high-risk pool program might be your best bet, because you can get in even if you have a preexisting condition. The program might not do much to make retiree insurance affordable to you, though. Under the new law, the risk pools can charge older people as much as four times more in premiums than they charge everyone else. At best, it might tide you over until the health insurance exchanges are available, in 2014. By then, you won't be able to be rejected for private insurance anymore, and your premiums can be only three times higher than everyone else's because of your age.

9

Medicare Changes

If you're on Medicare, or will be soon, you've probably heard a lot of things about the new law that completely contradict each other. One side has been saying that your Medicare coverage will be better than ever, with prescription drug coverage you can count on much more than you can now. The other side has been telling you the sky is falling, Medicare is being slashed, and Grandma is about to be pushed down the stairs in her wheelchair.

So let's all take a deep breath. The reality is the new law will make some of your benefits better, but it will also help pay for health care reform by making those cuts to Medicare that Congress thinks will be the least painful. So it's a bit like putting one foot on the accelerator and the other on the brake. On the bright side, you'll get a better prescription drug benefit—one that doesn't suddenly quit on you when you've spent too much. That part should help you a lot over time, but the gap in coverage won't be completely gone until 2020, so it might be a few years before you notice a big change. In the meantime, you're supposed to get brand-name drugs for half price while you're in that coverage gap.

But while that's happening, the new law will tighten the payments made to Medicare providers and to Medicare Advantage plans, the private plans that offer Medicare benefits. You can't do this and expect that nothing will happen. There may be a risk that some doctors will lose enough money that they might stop taking Medicare patients—which could make it harder for you to find a doctor to treat you. But we're not likely to see the worst predictions about the new law realized, and if there's real trouble, Congress probably will find a way to cancel or scale back the cuts, just as it has done in the past. And if you're in a Medicare Advantage plan, what you'll probably see is a bit less of the "extra" benefits, such as vision care and gym memberships. They're not cutting the things that could make the difference between life and death.

Your Prescription Drug Coverage

When Congress created the Medicare prescription drug program in 2003, it left a gaping hole in the area of drug benefits. This is the infamous "donut hole," and it's there because of one of those messy compromises that didn't even make much sense at the time. The Republicans who controlled Congress wanted to spend only a certain amount of money on drug coverage, but the Democrats wanted it to cover everyone, not just the seniors who had the least amount of money. So the compromise was to give everyone drug coverage, but only at the low end and high end of drug spending. In the middle, everyone would have to pay their own way.

What that means is that in 2010, without any change to the law, you would likely have faced a $3,610 gap in which you would have had to pay the drug costs yourself. Here's how it works, according to the Henry J. Kaiser Family Foundation: If you had the standard Medicare drug benefit, you would have paid a $310 deductible. After you paid off the deductible, you would have paid 25 percent of drug costs up to $2,830. After that, you would have had to pay for *all* of your drug bills until you had spent a total of $4,550 out of your own pocket. If you counted your own spending and your plan's coverage, that would have been a total of $6,440 in drug costs. If your drug bills got that high, you would have had to pay only 5 percent of the costs after that.

Shockingly, it turns out that people who get Medicare drug coverage don't like to find out there's such a big hole in it. In reality, you're not likely to spend enough to fall into the gap. Only about 14 percent of all of the people in the Medicare drug program hit it. Still, the whole idea of an incomplete drug program is a bit hard to defend. So the new law is going to phase out the "donut hole"—slowly, over a period of ten years.

It starts in 2010, when you'll get a $250 rebate if you hit the gap. Then, over the next ten years, a variety of discounts and subsidies will be phased in. You'll get a discount on brand-name drugs starting in 2011, subsidies for generic drugs beginning the same year, and more subsidies for brand-name drugs starting in 2013. The subsidies will increase over time. And by 2020, the combination should be enough to close the gap. You'll still have to pay a 25 percent coinsurance for both brand-name and generic drugs, but the rest should be covered.

Closing the "Donut Hole"

2010
$250 rebate

2011
50 percent discount on brand-name drugs
Generic drug subsidies begin

2013
50 percent discount on brand-name drugs
Generic drug subsidies increase
More subsidies for brand-name drugs begin

2020
Brand-name drugs
50 percent discount
Medicare covers 25 percent
You pay 25 percent

Generic drugs
Medicare covers 75 percent
You pay 25 percent

There's quite a political backstory behind the brand-name drug discounts. Beginning in 2011, the drug companies will have to give you a 50 percent discount on brand-name drugs you buy when you're in the donut hole—whether you buy them at a pharmacy or online. That's because the Pharmaceutical Research and Manufacturers of America, or PhRMA, volunteered to give everyone this discount as part of an agreement with the Obama administration and one of the Senate committees that wrote the law. So even while the donut hole still exists, you won't have to pay quite as much for those drugs as you would have otherwise.

As you can guess, PhRMA got something in return. The deal was that PhRMA would support health care reform, wouldn't try to shoot it down with negative ads, and would pitch in $80 billion worth of help for seniors' drug costs—if the Obama administration agreed not to try to cut any more than $80 billion from drug makers' revenues. That meant it could not support one of the most popular ideas for cutting drug costs: allowing people to buy prescription drugs from countries such as Canada, where they cost less. When Congress tried to add that idea to the bill, the Obama administration opposed it, and the idea failed. So even though you'll get some relief from drug prices, the fact that you won't get more relief—and the rest of us who buy prescription drugs won't, either—is the price we have to pay for the cease-fire the administration worked out with the powerful drug industry.

Other new benefits didn't come with such a high price tag. One of them is better preventive care. Starting in September 2010, you won't have to pay any coinsurance or deductibles for preventive benefits recommended by the U.S. Preventive Services Task Force. The task force rates different preventive screenings according to their effectiveness, and Medicare's new coverage will be restricted to services the task force has given a grade of A or B.

So you'll be covered for things such as screenings for high blood pressure, diabetes for adults with high blood pressure, and breast and colorectal cancer. Be warned, though: This is the same task force that took a beating for saying women in their forties should stop getting mammograms every year. So its recommendations aren't always going to cover the services that many medical experts recommend.

The Real Story of the Cuts

Over and over again, the opponents of the health care reform bill warned that it would cut Medicare drastically and lead to the rationing of health care for senior citizens. Neither is true. But it is true that, to help pay for health care reform, Congress will try to tighten Medicare spending in certain areas so it grows more slowly. So it's worth a closer look at exactly what will be cut and at the most reliable guesses as to what will happen.

For starters, the new law will attempt to save $136 billion over ten years by paying less to Medicare Advantage plans, which provide health care to about ten million people. The whole point of allowing private plans, such as HMOs or preferred provider organizations, to provide Medicare services was to get better use of the money than the old "fee-for-service" system, where doctors did whatever they wanted and Medicare just paid the bills. That's why, as far back as 1971, the federal government started allowing the private plans to participate. Over the years, Congress has started paying more to these private plans as a way to get more of them to take part in the program.

But by 2009, an investigation by the House Energy and Commerce Committee found that Medicare Advantage plans used more than 15 percent of your premiums for profits, marketing, high executive pay, and other expenses that had little to do with health care. (That doesn't compare well to the regular Medicare program, which spends 98 percent of your premiums on medical care.) If Medicare Advantage plans were spending that much of your money on overhead, congressional Democrats thought, they could stand to lose some of it without hurting your health care.

In 2009, the federal government was paying the Medicare Advantage plans $11 billion more than it would have paid to cover the same people under regular Medicare.

Here's how the cuts are supposed to work: Every Medicare Advantage plan currently submits a "bid" for how much it will spend to provide Medicare benefits to its customers. The government has its own formula for figuring out how much it expects to spend in your geographic area. If the plan's bid is lower than the amount it gets from the government, it can spend the leftover money on extra benefits for you. That's called a "rebate," and it's usually used for add-ons such as vision, hearing, or dental care, or to let you pay a lower cost for your regular Medicare benefits.

Under the new law, the government will change the formula so it pays less to the Medicare Advantage plans, especially in areas where providers get paid a lot for medical services. The cutbacks will be phased in starting in 2011, with most areas getting tighter payments over three years. For the areas with the deepest cuts, it will take six years. Not every plan will face cutbacks, and in fact, the plans with the highest quality ratings will get bonuses. But the goal is to tighten the screws on the plans that are clearly spending more of the taxpayers' money than they need to.

If you're in one of those plans, this probably means there will be smaller "rebates," and therefore less money for add-ons. But it shouldn't hurt the basic Medicare services you depend on. One prediction, by Richard S. Foster, the chief actuary for the agency that runs the Medicare program, sees the changes leading to "less generous benefit packages" for Medicare Advantage plans. Another, by the Congressional Budget Office, expects the value of the extra benefits to shrink, but not disappear.

If you're in a Medicare Advantage plan and you're worried about losing some of your extra benefits, you can switch plans between mid-November and early December every year, so that's a good time to look for another plan that might preserve more of the add-ons. You can compare the prices of different Medicare Advantage plans in your area, check the benefits, and look at some basic quality ratings at the official Medicare program Web site, www.medicare.gov.

It will be harder to predict what will happen when the new law tightens payments to Medicare providers. The Medicare program is already known for paying doctors and hospitals less than they get from private health insurance. Overall, Medicare's payments are about 80 percent of private insurance rates. Starting in 2010, the new law will increase Medicare's payments to some providers more slowly, including for inpatient hospital, home health, and skilled nursing facility services. These providers currently get increases in their payment rates each year, and the government will try to save $157 billion over ten years by increasing those payments by smaller amounts than before. The idea is to expect the providers to become more productive, giving you your medical care more efficiently than they used to.

The problem with expecting Medicare providers to get better across the board, of course, is that not all of them will. Some of them may not be able to, and some just won't bother. Either way, there's always a risk that when providers are paid less, some of them might just stop seeing Medicare patients altogether. Foster, the Medicare actuary, warned of this possibility, saying the payments made to providers might be slowed down to the point where they had little to do with what it actually cost to treat patients. The Congressional Budget Office basically shrugged off the question, saying it was "unclear" if providers would really become more efficient or if they'd give less care to Medicare patients.

Still, it's not as if the providers have no fat to cut. In testimony before a congressional panel in 2009, the chairman of the independent commission that advises Congress on Medicare payments said that even though some hospitals are losing money on Medicare, plenty of them are doing fine and the payments they receive from Medicare are "adequate to cover the costs of efficient hospitals." Besides, Medicare spending has been growing faster than the economy for years. That's also the case for all health care across the board, but Medicare has been growing faster than Medicaid or private health care spending. If there's any place where health care can become more efficient, Medicare is probably the best place to start.

The Pilot Programs

It's also a good place to start because Medicare has a strong influence on how private insurance pays doctors and hospitals in the rest of the health care system. Because of this fact, the new law sets up a whole series of experiments that will test new ways of paying Medicare providers and organizing their services. You might or might not run into them, because the Department of Health and Human Services still has to decide how widely they should be tried. But the point will be to find ways to spend less on medical care and try to make it more efficient.

These experiments will be described in more detail in Chapter 14, but here are the high points:

- One pilot program will test "bundled" payments for places such as skilled nursing facilities, long-term-care hospitals, and home health agencies, where the providers would be paid for a single episode of health care—such as a surgery or a heart attack—rather than for each separate service they provided.
- Another would try out "accountable care organizations," groups led by physicians—and organized around places such as hospitals or group practices—which would take on all the responsibility for the costs and quality of a patient's care. They would keep the savings if they can take care of their patients at lower costs than expected.
- Hospitals that treat Medicare patients will get financial rewards for treating expensive conditions well, and penalties if too many of their patients have to be readmitted for complications that we know how to prevent.

RESOURCES

For more information and advice on how to prepare for the changes, check out these resources as the Medicare changes kick in:

The **Medicare.gov** Web site (www.medicare.gov) is likely to post updates on the new law, and it's also a good place to look for the regulations the Medicare agency will put out later to fill in some of the details of the law. It also has several features that can help you do some of your own research and comparison shopping. It includes search tools to help you look for Medicare prescription drug plans, hospitals, Medigap policies to cover services that aren't covered by traditional Medicare, Medicare Advantage plans, nursing homes, and home health agencies. If you don't have Internet access, call 1-800-MEDICARE (1-800-633-4227) to get help over the phone or to order written materials.

State Health Insurance Counseling and Assistance Programs (SHIPs) can give you one-on-one counseling to talk you through your Medicare options, including whether to stick with regular Medicare or get a Medicare Advantage plan, how to understand your bill, and how to file an appeal if you're having a coverage problem. You can find the state programs through the Medicare.gov Web site or through the SHIP-Talk site (www.shiptalk.org).

The **Henry J. Kaiser Family Foundation** has a good explanation of how the prescription drug "donut hole" will be closed, with charts that can help you understand how much the gap will shrink each year. You can find it at www.kff.org/healthreform/upload/8059.pdf, or call the foundation at (650) 854-9400.

The **Medicare Rights Center** helps educate Medicare participants about how the system works and advises them on how to reduce their drug costs and resolve disputes. Their hotline number is 1-800-333-4114, and their Web site is www.medicarerights.org.

The **Center for Medicare Advocacy** provides education and legal assistance to people on Medicare. Based in Connecticut, its main phone number is (860) 456-7790, and the Web site is www.medicareadvocacy .org.

BenefitsCheckUp is a service run by the National Council on Aging to help you find assistance with your Medicare prescription drug coverage. The Web site is www.benefitscheckup.org, or call the council at (202) 479-1200.

10

The Expansion of Medicaid

If you're requiring everyone to get health coverage, you need to find a better place for people to go who aren't rolling in money. Otherwise, good luck. Congress knew this would be a problem, and that's why the new law will lead to a big expansion of Medicaid, the health care program for low-income people, the poor elderly, and people with disabilities. So if you're working hard and struggling to keep a roof over your head, you might have a better shot at getting Medicaid coverage than you did before.

Since it was created in 1965, Medicaid has been the main health care program for people with low incomes, and it's the biggest single source of health care for children throughout the country. It covers forty-four million people in low-income families, including twenty-nine million kids—a quarter of all of America's children. Most of the parents are working but don't earn nearly enough to get private health insurance. Low-income families are the biggest group of people in the program, but Medicaid also covers eight million people with disabilities, such as physical and mental problems. And it helps nine million senior citizens who are too poor to pay their Medicare premiums or who need help paying for long-term care.

The problem is, Medicaid has never covered *all* low-income people. If it did, there probably would be a lot fewer people without health insurance, because more people who worked at low-wage jobs would be able to get coverage. Unfortunately, up until now Medicaid has had specific, and fairly narrow, criteria for the groups of people who can get into the program. If you didn't fit into one of their categories, you usually were out of luck, unless your state decided to let more people in.

Under the old law, these are the groups of people who could get Medicaid coverage:

- Pregnant women and children under age 6, if their incomes were less than 133 percent of the federal poverty level. That's $29,327 a year for a family of four.
- Children between ages six and eighteen, in families with incomes up to the federal poverty level. That's $22,050 a year for a family of four.
- Parents who would have been eligible for their state's welfare programs as of 1996. (In a lot of cases, their income had to be less than half of the federal poverty level.)
- Senior citizens and people with disabilities who were also in the Supplemental Security Income program, which pays a small monthly income to those who need extra help.

This leaves out large groups of poor people, which helps explain why low-income adults are one of the largest groups of the uninsured. In fact, in many low-income families, the children are covered by Medicaid but the parents aren't. That's because even though all low-income kids can get Medicaid, that's not true for adults. Only about four out of ten adults under the poverty line have Medicaid coverage. And if you're a poor adult without kids, you can't get Medicaid at all, unless you're a pregnant mother-to-be or you have a disability. This is a big reason why more than a third of all poor people have no health coverage—not counting senior citizens—and nearly a third of all people with incomes between the poverty line and twice the poverty line are uninsured.

The states have a bit of leeway to cover more people or provide more benefits. Medicaid is funded by both the federal government and the states, and even though the federal government sets the general rules, the states can go beyond them in a lot of ways and still get federal funds. As long as the economy is in bad shape, though, states aren't going to do anything more than they absolutely have to. They're having a hard enough time with their budgets as it is.

So if Congress wanted to make its new "everyone has to get health coverage" rule anything more than a cruel joke, it had to give struggling people an easier way to afford it. Many will be able to get private health insurance with the subsidies we discussed in Chapter 4. But for a lot of people, private health insurance will always be too expensive, even with the subsidies. If you want to reach a lot of low-income people quickly, a bigger Medicaid program is the quickest way to do it. So that's the way the authors of the new law decided to go.

Who Will Get In

In a few years, Medicaid will be open to everyone with incomes up to 133 percent of the federal poverty line. That means more parents and more children will be able to get Medicaid coverage. And for the first time, it will be open even to low-income adults who don't have kids and don't have a disability. As of 2010, 133 percent of the federal poverty line is $14,404 for one person, and $29,327 a year for a family of four. But those income levels will probably go up a bit by the time the new rules kick in.

They're also going to make it a bit easier to apply by taking away the asset tests that you used to have to go through—the painful documentation of all of your resources other than your home—unless you're trying to get long-term-care coverage. After these changes take effect, there could be as many as sixteen million more people receiving coverage through Medicaid and the State Children's Health Insurance Program, a similar program that covers children in families that earn too much for Medicaid but can't afford private insurance.

Change	Effective Date
States can choose to begin the expanded coverage early	2011
All states have to provide the expanded coverage	2014

Who Will Pay for It

Usually the federal government and the states split the costs of Medicaid. This varies from state to state, but in general, the federal government pays anywhere from half to three quarters of the costs. But in order to bring more people into Medicaid without bankrupting the states, Congress had to offer to have the federal government pick up the whole check—at least for the first few years.

So between 2014 and 2016, the federal government will pay all of the costs for the new people on Medicaid. After that, the federal funds will be phased back a bit each year. By 2020, the federal government will pick up only 90 percent of the costs, and the states will have to pay the rest. There will also be extra federal help for states that already were covering adults without children, since those states argued that it was unfair to give all the help to other states that hadn't been as generous.

You may have heard that one state, Nebraska, was supposed to get a special deal where the federal government would keep paying for all of the new people on the state's Medicaid rolls and the state wouldn't have to pay anything. That's because the Democrats in the Senate badly needed the vote of one of their last holdouts, Ben Nelson of Nebraska, to have enough votes to pass the health care reform bill. Nelson was able to name his price, and extra Medicaid help for his state was part of that price.

Once the public found out about this, however, there was a huge uproar. The deal became known as the "Cornhusker Kickback," and it gave the bill's critics an excuse to charge that the whole bill was full of such backroom deals. The episode embarrassed nearly everyone in Congress, including Nelson, who insisted he never meant for Nebraska to be the only state that got help. So the deal isn't there anymore. In the final bill, the version that Obama signed into law, Congress took it out.

How to Sign Up

Soon you'll be able to apply for Medicaid at places other than Medicaid and welfare offices. As soon as the new health insurance exchanges are available in 2014—the same year Medicaid is expanded—you'll be able to sign up there, too. There will be a standard form that you can fill out in person, online, by mail, or over the phone.

> Starting in 2014, if you apply for any kind of coverage through your state's health insurance exchange, they're supposed to check to see if you qualify for either Medicaid or the State Children's Health Insurance Program. If you do, they'll enroll you automatically.

If you can't wait until 2014, check with your state Medicaid agency to see if you qualify now, or if they're one of the states that might expand its coverage early. A complete list of state Medicaid agencies, including their phone numbers and Web sites, is included in the appendix to this book. In some cases, they might direct you to your regional office, which is often the better place to sign up.

What You Get Through Medicaid

There is a set of benefits that you have to get no matter what state you're in, and then there's another set of benefits that aren't required but that a lot of states provide anyway. Here are the main ones you have to get in every state:

- Doctors' visits
- Hospital services
- Laboratory tests and X-rays
- Community health center services
- Family planning
- Pediatrician visits
- Nursing homes for people over age twenty-one
- Home health care

If you have children, they get another set of services that are very important. These are called Early and Periodic Screening, Diagnosis, and Treatment (EPSDT) services, and they include physical exams, immunizations, full histories of your child's physical and mental health development, vision care, hearing exams, dental care, and a wide range of treatments for physical or mental health problems. It's considered better coverage than a lot of children get through private health insurance.

There is another set of benefits that states don't have to give you, but many of them do anyway. For example, you should be able to get prescription drug coverage in every state, even though it isn't required. You're also likely to get other valuable benefits such as clinic services, dental care, eyeglasses, rehabilitation, and personal care services. For all of these benefits, you'll get the full coverage only if they're considered "medically necessary." Different states have different ideas on what is necessary, and if you get your health care through managed care, they might have their own definition, too.

You get most of these benefits at a lot lower cost than most people pay under private insurance. You can't be charged a monthly premium, for example, unless your income is over 150 percent of the federal poverty line. Adults can be charged small deductibles, such as $2 a month; small copayments of $3 or less; and coinsurance payments. You're just not supposed to pay more than 5 percent of your annual income. In most cases, children and pregnant women don't have to pay any of this. Anyone can be charged, however, if they use the emergency room when it's not an emergency.

Trouble Finding a Doctor

One of the biggest problems with Medicaid, as you know if you're already in it, is that it can be a challenge to find a doctor who will take you. That's because Medicaid is well known among doctors and hospitals for paying low rates for services. Some states pay more than others, but on average, Medicaid pays primary care providers only about two thirds of what they get from Medicare. This says a lot, because Medicare already pays a fair amount less than private insurance.

So if you sign up for Medicaid, you'll be more protected from big health care costs than you were before, but just be aware that you may not be able to find doctors as easily as people with private health coverage. The new law is trying to do something about this problem, by raising Medicaid's rates so it pays primary care providers as much as Medicare in 2013 and 2014. The federal government will pick up the check for this, so your state shouldn't have any trouble even if it is in the middle of a budget crunch. It's just a temporary fix, though, since it lasts for only two years.

Preventive Care

If you're already in the Medicaid program, the new law is trying to give you better preventive care to keep you from getting sick. Starting in 2013, your state will get extra federal money if it covers preventive services without making you share the costs. These would have to be services recommended by the U.S. Preventive Services Task Force or adult immunizations endorsed by the federal Advisory Committee on Immunization Practices. If your state decides to add the preventive coverage, you will get better access to services such as screenings for high blood pressure and counseling for obesity, screenings for hearing loss in newborn infants and depression in teenagers, and seasonal flu vaccinations for adults. Check with your state Medicaid agency to see if it plans to add the coverage.

Starting in October 2010, state Medicaid programs will have to cover programs to help pregnant women stop smoking. And beginning in 2011, your state can get federal grants to encourage people to enroll in programs to prevent chronic conditions such as obesity, high cholesterol, high blood pressure, and diabetes.

The State Children's Health Insurance Program

Another option, if you have children and earn a bit too much to qualify for Medicaid, is to enroll your children in the State Children's Health

Insurance Program, or SCHIP. Like Medicaid, SCHIP is funded by both the federal government and the states, and provides coverage for kids in low-income families—sometimes through Medicaid, and sometimes through separate programs. The new law guarantees that SCHIP will be funded through 2015, and the states will get extra federal funds starting in 2014. It also declares that states can't change their eligibility standards until 2019. This means the states can't try to save money by making it harder for people to enroll their children in the program.

The program is safe for now, but some members of Congress had hoped to end SCHIP and move the children enrolled in it into the new health insurance exchanges. The problem is, the kinds of private plans that will participate in the exchanges aren't likely to cover children nearly as well as SCHIP. A study conducted by the consulting firm Watson Wyatt Worldwide found that an average family at 225 percent of the federal poverty line—about $41,200 for a family of three—would pay nearly $1,200 in premiums and out-of-pocket expenses to cover one child in a typical "silver" plan in the state exchanges. That's nearly twice as much as they would have paid in the SCHIP programs in Maryland, Pennsylvania, and West Virginia, the three most expensive programs it studied at that income level.

So by April 1, 2015, the Department of Health and Human Services is supposed to declare which exchange plans in each state, if any, offer children's benefits that are as good, and at about the same cost to parents, as the state SCHIP program. Until then, the states are not supposed to "dump" low-income children into the exchanges. However, this may not be enough to prevent states from putting a freeze on enrollment. That's what Arizona did in March 2010, and other states have permission to do so if they run out of state funds.

Since we don't know how many states might stop taking new applications—and some states have waiting periods anyway—your best bet is to apply for your state's SCHIP program as soon as possible.

To find out if you qualify for it, check the Insure Kids Now Web site (www.insurekidsnow.gov), or start with your state's Medicaid agency (listed in the appendix). It's also a good idea to apply for Medicaid, just in case you qualify, since it doesn't have waiting lists.

Alternative State Plans

There is another option that some states might use to cover people who are just outside the reach of Medicaid. States will be able to contract with private health plans to set up a basic health care program for people between 133 percent and 200 percent of the federal poverty line. That's individuals earning between $14,404 and $21,660 a year or a family of four with an income between $29,326 and $44,100 a year. At press time, it was not clear how many states might set up this kind of program.

Legal Immigrants

Under federal law, legal immigrants can't get coverage through either Medicaid or SCHIP until they have been in the country for five years. If you're in this category, you will still have to wait, as the new health care law doesn't change the waiting period. However, you should be able to get private coverage through the new health insurance exchanges. And if your state sets up a basic health care program through a private health plan, you should be able to use it if your income is below 200 percent of the federal poverty line—$21,660 a year for an individual and $44,100 a year for a family of four.

RESOURCES

Although it should become easier to apply for Medicaid once the exchanges are available, you can start by getting information from your state Medicaid agency or from the regional office in your area. A list of **state Medicaid agencies** is included in the appendix to this book. Some of them can give you information about how to apply online or by phone. In other cases, they will direct you to the regional office where you can sign up.

If you run into trouble applying, your local **legal services office** may be able to help you. A list of legal services organizations by state and county is available through the Web site of the **Legal Services Corporation,** a nonprofit corporation that provides legal aid to low-income people. You can find the list at www.rin.lsc.gov/scripts/LSC/PD/PDList7.asp. Once you have found a legal services organization in your area, you can look up their Web site to find the office closest to you. If you don't have Internet access, call the Legal Services Corporation at (202) 295-1500.

If you can't get into either Medicaid or the State Children's Health Insurance Program, your best bet—until the new health insurance exchanges open in 2014—is to look for a **community health center** in your area. These federally funded health centers are set up to help you get primary care if you have no health coverage or if the coverage you have is not enough to meet your needs. They're usually located in urban or rural areas where people have a hard time finding primary care. You can find a health center in your area through a Web site run by the Health Resources and Services Administration, www.findahealthcenter .hrsa.gov/.

11

Long-Term Care

For the most part, the issue of how to help people with long-term care stayed under the radar during the health care reform debate. There was some talk about a new long-term-care coverage program that would be created by the new law, though it was mostly a partisan debate about whether it would break the bank. Otherwise, you wouldn't have known Congress was even paying attention. That's a shame, because one of the most emotional and complicated issues we'll all face is how to take care of our loved ones when they get older—and how to make sure they're in good hands.

Fortunately, there are parts of the new law that try to sort out the complexities of long-term care and make it a bit easier to pay for it. For people who have never had long-term care insurance—and really, that's most of us—there's a new program that will allow you to sign up through your workplace for basic insurance that can help with some of your long-term-care needs. There are also new standards that should allow you to research nursing homes more easily, if that's where a family member needs to go, and will try to make sure their staff are better trained and better screened.

Since Medicaid always has been the way most people get their long-term care, the new law will encourage states to let Medicaid pay for personal attendants and other kinds of at-home care, not just nursing homes. There's a lot at stake in finding the best ways to take care of seniors and people with lifelong disabilities; and finding facilities and caretakers you can trust, and the right supports to help family members live at home, will always be a complicated task. But the new law may give you some new options, and better information to help you make the best decisions.

The CLASS Independence Benefit Plan

The part of the law that creates a new insurance program for the elderly is called the Community Living Assistance Services and Supports Act, or CLASS Act. It's considered the legacy of the late senator Ted Kennedy, who wanted to give people a way to get basic long-term-care coverage more cheaply than they could in the private market. It's a voluntary insurance program that you'll be able to get through the workplace, and it will have to pay for itself through the premiums that will be deducted from your paycheck.

Here's how it will work: Starting in January 2011, if your employer decides to participate, the company will automatically sign you up for the new insurance program, which will be called the CLASS Independence Benefit Plan. But they'll have to tell you they did that and give you a chance to say no thanks if you don't want it. After you've paid the premiums for five years, you'll be eligible for a cash benefit to use when you get older if you become unable to perform at least two or three "activities of daily living" on your own (such as feeding, dressing, or bathing yourself).

Under the new voluntary long-term-care coverage program, you'd get at least $50 a day in benefits, depending on how serious your mental or physical limitations are. You would pay the premiums through payroll deductions, and you would have to pay into the program for at least five years before collecting on it.

You'll have a pretty wide range of options for what to do with the money. If you want to keep living at home, you'll be able to spend it on personal assistance, home care, nursing support, modifications to your home, transportation, technology to help you with everyday activities, or respite care to give relief to whoever has been taking care of you. If you need to be in a hospital or nursing home, you'll be able to use the money to help you with those costs. You'll also be able to get advocacy services, if you're having trouble with your care, and advice on what kind of care would make the most sense for you.

If you heard about this program at all during the debate in Congress, it was probably because of the charges that the CLASS Act would become just another expensive entitlement, sucking up more and more government money the way Medicare and Medicaid have. Actually, it's supposed to pay for itself over the long run. In fact, the new law requires the Department of Health and Human Services to design the program in a way that keeps its funds stable seventy-five years into the future. How it will do that, exactly, is one of several key details about the law Congress has left blank. The Department of Health and Human Services will have to fill those in later. HHS has to set the premiums, raise them if the program isn't paying for itself, and figure out how to let you sign up if your employer doesn't want to take part in the program.

The real question, though, is whether enough people will sign up for the program to allow it to pay for itself. Since there's no rule requiring people to join it, it could run into the same problem health insurance sometimes does: If the only people who join the program are the ones with ongoing and expensive health problems, and it doesn't have enough healthy people paying into it, it might have to charge higher premiums to cover its costs. And if the premiums become too expensive, people might be discouraged from signing up for the program. Private long-term-care insurance is already so costly—an average of $1,800 a year if you start in your forties, rising to $2,500 once you reach age sixty-five—that most people don't buy it. If this new coverage isn't cheaper than that, people might not buy it, either.

There's no way to know until the program is under way. If its price turns out to be something you think you can afford, it might be a smart choice for you to join it. That way, if you ever do become disabled in an accident or need assistance as you get older to remain independent, you will be able to draw down cash benefits to offset your costs. Remember that the younger you are when you join, the lower the premium will be, and the more people there are in the program, the more stable and successful it's likely to be. If the premiums rise too fast and you don't think you can afford it, you'll be able to cancel for a while and see if things improve. Just don't stay out too long if you think you might want to get back in, because you'll pay higher premiums when you rejoin. That's how they're going to discourage people from dropping in and out too much.

The other thing to keep in mind is that the new program won't give you enough coverage to be a substitute for private long-term-care insurance. If you get $50 a day through the program, that won't pay for a semi-private room in a nursing home (average cost: $198 a day), and it will cover only short visits from a home health aide (average cost: $21 an hour). So it's best to think of CLASS as a way to offset some of your costs, not eliminate them. If you want to be completely covered, you may still need some kind of private long-term-care insurance to fill in the gaps. Or you can rely on Medicaid, but you'll have to spend just about all of your assets to get it. That's exactly the kind of situation the CLASS Act is supposed to prevent.

If you're going to look into private long-term-care insurance as an add-on to the CLASS Act program, be aware that the policies can have a lot of loopholes, because some states regulate them more strictly than others. Rate increases can be a problem, too. Some states have fairly strict rules about keeping long-term-care insurance premiums from going up too much, but others don't do much to make sure insurance companies keep the rates reasonable. Finally, long-term-care insurance isn't always a smart use of your money. It can be, if you have a lot of money and assets to protect, but it doesn't make sense if you don't have much money and might not be able to afford the premium.

Some senators are already talking about stronger standards for long-term-care insurance, as a follow-up now that the new health care law is in place. In the meantime, you should learn as much as you can about long-term-care insurance and look at the coverage closely before you decide to buy anything. The National Association of Insurance Commissioners, which develops consumer protection standards that states can use as models for their laws, has some good advice about what questions to ask and what to watch out for. You can find the long-term-care section of the association's Web site at www.naic.org/index_ltc_section.htm.

New Nursing Home Rules

In the meantime, the new law tries to impose stronger standards on long-term care itself. Some of these should help you get better information on nursing homes when you're researching to find the best place for a member of your family. Others are more for the use of the regulators who are supposed to hold nursing home operators accountable when they don't take care of their patients. If these new standards work, you should find it a little bit easier to find a nursing facility that deserves your trust.

Here are the high points:

Full Disclosure

Skilled nursing facilities have to disclose more information about their ownership. Some of the more troubling problems with nursing homes in recent years have been traced to the private investment companies that buy them. They drain funds away that should be used to hire enough staff and keep the facilities clean and safe. Then, when the nursing home residents suffer and the regulators try to find out who is responsible, the companies create such complicated corporate structures that it's hard to tell who should be punished. The new health care law requires nursing homes to report more detailed ownership information to federal and state regulators, who in turn have to make it available to the public.

Compliance and Ethics Program

Nursing facilities have to put a compliance and ethics program in place within three years. This is the latest chapter in an ongoing battle to get nursing homes to explain how, exactly, they'll make sure all their employees follow all of the laws and rules. Otherwise, the worst facilities can deny that they ever had a plan, and the stories of financial fraud and the neglect of nursing home residents can continue. The Department of Health and Human Services is supposed to give the nursing homes some guidance on how to draw up these plans, and it might make available a "model" compliance program the facilities can use to design their own.

More Information on the Nursing Home Compare Web Site

This is part of the Medicare.gov Web site, run by the Department of Health and Human Services, that lets you look up quality information and inspection reports for nursing homes throughout the country. Right now it's not always easy to spot the homes with the biggest problems. Under the new law, the Web site will have to let you look up more information about the facilities' staffing levels, including how many hours of care each one gives its residents every day and how much staff turnover they've had. You'll also be able to research how many complaints they've had and how those issues were resolved, and whether there have been any criminal violations by the facilities or their employees.

More Detailed Pay Reporting Requirements

Skilled nursing facilities will have to report more details on the salaries and wages they pay to their staff. They'll have to break down the information so you can tell how many specialized staff they have on hand to deal with complex medical conditions such as Alzheimer's and other forms of dementia, and how many registered nurses and certified nurse assistants they have on hand.

Incentives to Report Their Own Problems

If nursing facilities are honest enough to admit their problems, and fix them within ten days after they happen, they can cut any potential fines in half. Congress is hoping this will be enough of an incentive to get more facilities to come forward, rather than hope no one finds out about their problems.

Monitoring of the Chains

There will be a pilot program in which an "independent monitor" will oversee big nursing home chains that operate within and between states. If the monitor finds problems and reports them to the chains, they have to find a way to fix them within ten days.

Advance Notice of Closings

Anytime a nursing facility closes, it can create chaos and anxiety for the residents and their families. The new law will require nursing home operators to give sixty days' notice if they're going to close a facility. And the state will have to come up with a plan for transferring the residents to other facilities that fit their needs. This doesn't guarantee a smooth transition, since there are sure to be situations where residents and their families don't agree with where the state wants to send patients. But these kinds of closings might at least become a bit more manageable than they are now.

Dementia Management and Abuse Prevention Training

It's not always clear how much the nursing staff knows about dealing with residents suffering from dementia, an emotionally devastating disease that has to be treated with dignity and respect. Staff members who aren't well prepared may be tempted to ignore residents' wishes and make decisions for them. The new law will require nursing homes to train new staff members in how to deal with dementia and prevent abuse before those employees start their jobs.

Background Checks

There will be a new program of national and state background checks to make sure no facility hires a worker who has abused patients or residents at another facility. The background checks would be used at places such as nursing homes, assisted living facilities, and home health agencies, and for providers of hospice care and personal attendant services.

New Medicaid Rules

Medicaid is by far the most common way people get their long-term care. It pays for 40 percent of all long-term-care spending in the country, and it's the way more than six out of ten nursing home residents pay for their care. Unfortunately, Medicaid's coverage rules are a bit out of date, so the state programs tend to steer people toward nursing homes rather than letting them stay at home or in their communities. That's not the way most seniors and others with lifelong disabilities would like to get their care. They'd like to stay as independent as possible, which is all that any of us wants out of life. If it were a bit easier for them to get the help they needed while staying at home, they'd prefer to do that. And in the long run, it would be cheaper for Medicaid to pay for that kind of care rather than expensive nursing homes.

So the new law makes a couple of changes that might allow more seniors to live the way they'd like to live. One part of the law, which takes effect in October 2011, will give states extra federal funds if they change their Medicaid rules to pay for more attendant services to help people live at home. This way, people could use Medicaid to hire attendants to help them take care of their "activities of daily living," such as dressing, eating, and bathing, and other chores, such as cooking meals and shopping for groceries. They could also pay for support services such as medical alert pagers in case they run into trouble.

There's also a change in the Medicaid rules that lets states offer home-based and community-based care to people with higher incomes—up to three times the benefit rate for Supplemental Security Income, or a total of $2,022 a month—and open up the range of services they could get. Your state's Medicaid program will have to decide whether to take advantage of the new rules to offer these services. If you or a member of your family is interested in exploring these options, check with your state's Medicaid agency to see if it is going to offer them. A full list of state Medicaid agency phone numbers and Web addresses is included in the appendix.

RESOURCES

The **Department of Health and Human Services** will have to fill in a lot of the details on the CLASS Act and the new nursing home standards. It will do this by issuing regulations, which are the lengthy sets of rules that agencies put out on how they will carry out new laws. They're usually technical and mind-numbingly boring, but they will explain some of the important points the law doesn't address, such as how HHS will set the premiums for the CLASS Act and what it will do to make sure you can sign up if your employer doesn't offer the coverage to you. There probably will be summaries that will be easier to read, too. Keep checking the department's Web site, www.hhs.gov, for updates.

The **Nursing Home Compare** section of the Medicare.gov Web site, the official site of the Medicare program, allows you to research quality ratings, inspection reports, and staff data for every Medicare- and Medicaid-certified nursing home in the country. The address is www.medicare.gov/NHCompare. You can also call the Centers for Medicare & Medicaid Services at 1-800-MEDICARE.

The **National Clearinghouse for Long-Term Care Information,** run by the Federal Administration on Aging, provides advice on how long-term care works, how to plan for your needs, and how to pay for them. The address is www.longtermcare.gov, or contact the Administration on Aging at (202) 619-0724.

The **National Long-Term Care Ombudsman Resource Center** has an interactive map on its Web site that can help you find the ombudsman closest to you. Long-term-care ombudsmen can help you resolve problems with nursing homes and learn about what kinds of rights the residents have. They may also know if a nursing facility you're considering has had a good track record or a history of troubles. The Web site is www.ltcombudsman.org, and you can contact the center at (202) 332-2275.

The **Eldercare Locator,** run by the Federal Administration on Aging, can help you find a local agency in your area that can connect you with home-based and community-based care services. You can search by city, county, or zip code to find the agency that can help you set up home care and help with meals and transportation. The site also has links to many other helpful resources, such as organizations with information on end-of-life care, living options, mental health services, and support for caregivers. The Web site is www.eldercare.gov, or call 1-800-677-1116.

12

Preventive Care and Wellness

Thousands of people die each year from conditions that could have been avoided if they had gotten the right screenings and guidance on how to take care of themselves. This is not a matter of debate—it's a fact that has been established in all of the latest medical research. They don't get the screenings and advice they need because our health care system hasn't given them enough of a reason to do so. Doctors have been trained to treat us when we're already sick, but many are so busy that they can't spend as much time on care that could keep us from getting sick in the first place. And our health coverage doesn't always pay well for that kind of care, so there's less of a reason for them to offer it—and less of a reason for most of us to seek it out.

So Congress wrote some measures into the new law that are supposed to encourage doctors and patients to take preventive care more seriously. By requiring private health insurance plans and Medicare to cover certain preventive services without making you share the cost, lawmakers are hoping that you'll be more likely to go in for the kinds of screenings that could keep you healthy. And by funding more kinds of prevention programs throughout the country, they're hoping this kind of care will be easier to find. If so, we might do better as a country at heading off serious illnesses that we know how to prevent.

As good as our health care is, we have been a lot better about finding out what prevents illnesses than actually doing it. According to a 2007 study by the Partnership for Prevention, a group of businesses, nonprofits, and government agencies that promotes preventive care, here are some of the steps we could easily take to avoid serious health problems:

- If 90 percent of adults took aspirin every day to prevent heart disease, we could save forty-five thousand Americans' lives each year. Right now, only half of all adults do this.
- If 90 percent of smokers got help to quit smoking, we could save forty-two thousand lives each year. Fewer than three out of ten smokers get that kind of help.
- If 90 percent of adults age fifty and older got colorectal cancer screenings, we could save fourteen thousand lives every year. Fewer than half are up to date on those screenings.
- If 90 percent of adults age fifty and older got the flu shot every year, we could save twelve thousand lives each year. Fewer than four out of ten get the shots.
- If 90 percent of all women age forty and older got breast cancer screenings every two years, we could save thirty-seven hundred lives every year. Only about two thirds of women get the screenings as often as they should.

However, in a health care system that is geared toward treating illness rather than preventing it, we don't put enough emphasis on getting the right treatment to the people who are at risk for conditions such as heart disease and cancer. And many of the people who are in danger of developing these conditions have no idea they're at risk, so they don't seek treatment. The other issue is that employers don't have a strong incentive to give their employees good preventive and wellness care. Some do, because they recognize that they get more work out of them if they stay healthy. But others don't see the point in covering preventive services that might not have any payoff until after the worker has moved on to another company.

If the new law succeeds in getting preventive care to more people, it's sure to save lives. It's less certain to save money. Some of the top Democrats in Congress were convinced that better preventive care would save money over the long run—because it's more expensive to treat the diseases than to keep them from developing—and that's why they pushed so hard for the new incentives. But the Congressional Budget Office said it was just as likely that the new benefits could just spend money on people who don't need it. Most of the independent research on preventive care finds that it can save money if the people at the highest risk for disease get the right help, but it's not a good use of money if a lot of it is spent on people who aren't in danger.

Still, most researchers conclude that saving lives is a good enough reason to fund preventive care and wellness programs. So if the number of deaths by these kinds of avoidable illnesses decreases over the years, this part of the law will likely be considered a success.

The New Prevention and Wellness Incentives

Here are the highlights of the new rules:

Preventive Services Covered at No Cost

All new private health insurance plans will have to cover preventive services without making you share the costs. They won't have to cover just anything, though—only the services that are recommended by official panels: screenings recommended by the U.S. Preventive Services Task Force, immunizations endorsed by the Centers for Disease Control and Prevention's Advisory Committee on Immunization Practices, children's screenings recommended by the Health Resources and Services Administration, and women's preventive care and screening services endorsed by the Health Resources and Services Administration. When new recommendations come out, the plans will have to start covering them within the next year.

So, starting in September 2010, you'll have the benefit of getting cheaper access to services such as screenings for high blood pressure, dietary counseling if you're at risk for heart disease, and annual flu shots. But you won't be guaranteed coverage of services such as prostate cancer screenings, since the Preventive Services Task Force says there's not enough evidence that the benefits of the tests outweigh the risks. Your health insurance company will be able to go beyond the official guidelines if it wants to, but it doesn't have to.

And there are bound to be controversies over what these official panels do and don't recommend. As if to prove the point, the law specifically says that the Preventive Services Task Force's least popular recommendation—that women in their forties stop getting mammograms—won't count in the new guidelines. Congress will just pretend it never happened.

> The law says your new preventive coverage of breast cancer screenings will be based on all of the Preventive Services Task Force's guidelines "other than those issued in or around November 2009." That was the one that said women in their forties don't need to get mammograms.

Better Medicare Coverage of Preventive Services

Starting in 2011, you'll get a free wellness visit with your physician once a year, and you and your physician will be able to come up with a personalized prevention plan for you. This can include things such as a screening schedule for the next five to ten years, a list of any risk factors or conditions you have and advice on how to treat them, and referrals to other medical professionals. You'll also be able to get preventive services without having to share any of the cost. These will include those services recommended with a grade of at least A or B by the Preventive Services Task Force, such as colorectal cancer screenings for seniors (only until age seventy-five), screenings for high blood pressure, and testing for Type 2 diabetes in people with high blood pressure.

Medicaid Coverage of Programs for Pregnant Women

As of October 2010, if you're on Medicaid, you will not have to pay any share of the costs for antitobacco programs for pregnant women. They have to be services recommended by the U.S. Public Health Service, and they have to be supervised by a physician or other medical professional.

New Incentives for Medicaid Coverage of Preventive Care

They won't have to offer you the coverage, but they will get extra federal funds if they choose to cover the preventive services recommended by the U.S. Preventive Services Task Force and the adult immunizations recommended by the CDC's Advisory Committee on Immunization Practices. If your state covers these services, you won't have to share any of the costs. You can find out more by contacting your state Medicaid agency through the list in the appendix.

More Funding for School-Based Health Centers

Between now and 2013, there will be $50 million a year available to help your community set up school-based health centers. These are places where children and adolescents get preventive and primary care in communities where these services are hard to find. There is not a lot of detail yet on how many more centers will become available or how quickly, but more information should be available after the Department of Health and Human Services puts out additional guidance. You can check the Web site of the National Assembly on School-Based Health Care, www.nasbhc.org, for updates.

New Fund for Preventive Care and Public Health Services

The law creates a Prevention and Public Health Fund to provide, for the first time, a stable source of federal money for prevention, wellness, and public health programs. Starting in 2010, it will get $500 million, a figure that will rise to $2 billion a year by 2015. This will help support initiatives such as immunization programs, educational campaigns on the benefits of preventive care, and new grants to help communities launch their own programs to prevent chronic diseases.

Nutrition Labeling

Starting in 2011, any restaurant chain with twenty or more locations will have to list on their menus the calories for everything they serve. Vending machines would have to list calories, too. And if you ask for it, chain restaurants will also have to give you a written list of other nutritional information for their food, such as how much fat, saturated fat, cholesterol, sodium, carbohydrates, sugars, dietary fiber, and protein you'll find in everything on the menu. This way, you can still buy that super jumbo bacon double cheeseburger with extra grease, but you can't say nobody warned you about it.

Incentive	Effective Date
Coverage in private plans	September 23, 2010
Medicare coverage	January 1, 2011
Medicaid	
• Coverage of antitobacco services for pregnant women	October 1, 2010
• Optional state coverage of other preventive services	January 1, 2013
Prevention and Public Health Fund	Funding begins in 2010

RESOURCES

The **U.S. Preventive Services Task Force,** a sixteen-member panel of primary care physicians that reviews medical evidence on the effectiveness of preventive services, will be the source of most of the recommendations for what the new health care plans and programs will have to cover. You can check their latest list of recommendations at www .ahrq.gov/CLINIC/uspstfix.htm. If you don't have Internet access, you can also get information by calling the Agency for Healthcare Research and Quality, which sponsors the task force, at (301) 427-1364.

The **Advisory Committee on Immunization Practices,** a fifteen-member panel that operates under the Centers for Disease Control and Prevention, makes the official federal recommendations on what vaccines should be given to adults and children. You can get information on vaccine policies, available in English and Spanish, by calling 1-800-232-4636.

You can also read the panel's recommendations at www.cdc.gov/vaccines/recs/ACIP. Warning: They're really, really technical.

Bright Futures, a project of the Maternal and Child Health Bureau of the Health Resources and Services Administration, has collaborated with the American Academy of Pediatrics on a set of recommendations for preventive care for infants, children, and adolescents. You can find them at www.brightfutures.aap.org, under the "Clinical Practices" tab. You can also call the American Academy of Pediatrics at (847) 434-4000.

The **Partnership for Prevention,** the coalition of businesses, nonprofits, and government agencies that promotes preventive care, offers reports on the effectiveness of different kinds of preventive care and advice for employers who want to start covering those services. The group can be reached at (202) 833-0009 or www.prevent.org.

13

Who Decides What Care
You Get?

There's nothing scarier than the thought of a government bureaucracy making medical decisions for you and your doctor. Especially if it's that guy from the Department of Motor Vehicles who acts like he doesn't care about anything. Or that automated phone switchboard that tells you to "Press Five" and then hangs up on you. Fortunately, the new law isn't going to put these kinds of cartoon characters in charge of your health care. Instead, it gives the federal government a lot of power to crack down on bad health insurance practices, give you new benefits, and test new practices that might help us figure out how to spend our health care money more wisely. It doesn't mean the government will actually become your doctor.

So why did you hear so much talk during the congressional debate about "government making medical decisions"? This charge wasn't made up out of thin air—for the most part. Instead, it was based on wildly distorted or exaggerated readings of different versions of the bill. What connects all of the charges is the fear that, in its zeal to bring down health care costs, the federal government will deny you the medical care you need. It is true, as we'll see in Chapter 14, that we spend too much on health care, and that's a big part of the reason our premiums keep rising by ridiculous amounts every year. Someday we'll all have to have a grown-up conversation about how to focus more on what we really need and not just what we'd like to have.

But despite what you may have heard, the new law doesn't do very much to march us down that road. So let's pause and walk through the charges, compare them to what the bill actually says, and then you can decide how scared you want to be.

Death Panels

There aren't any, but here's why you've heard about them. Back in July 2009, Betsy McCaughey, who rose to fame as a critic of Bill Clinton's health care plan in 1994 and later became the lieutenant governor of New York, decided that part of the original House bill called for a "required counseling session" for everyone on Medicare that would "tell them how to end their life sooner." Actually, what the bill said was that people on Medicare who wanted to talk to doctors about end-of-life care could do it and Medicare would pay for it. This would have allowed people to get advice on how to draw up a living will—which lets you tell your doctors how aggressively they should try to save your life if you're gravely ill and can't tell them yourself—and what other kinds of end-of-life services would be available.

It's a serious subject, and it deserves an adult conversation. According to a study published in *The New England Journal of Medicine* in April 2010, 42 percent of adults over age sixty have to make some kind of decision about their end-of-life care, and 70 percent of them are no longer capable of doing so. But the idea that Congress was trying to cut off health care for old people caught on. The "death panels" phrase came from Sarah Palin, who wrote in an August 2009 Facebook post,

"The America I know and love is not one in which my parents or my baby with Down Syndrome will have to stand in front of Obama's 'death panel' so his bureaucrats can decide, based on a subjective judgment of their 'level of productivity in society,' whether they are worthy of health care."

Soon members of Congress were getting questions about "death panels" at town hall meetings. The House changed its bill's language to say repeatedly that the counseling sessions would be "voluntary." The Senate didn't even put the language in its bill. And it's not in the new law.

Deciding What Benefits You Get

This came up a lot, as it did in House Minority Leader John Boehner's closing speech just before the House voted on the bill in November 2009. Boehner went through a lengthy list of all the powers the federal government would have under the bill. He was especially critical of the role of what he called the "health czar," the Health Choices Commissioner who would have carried out most of the reforms under the House bill. (Don't look for this position in the law; it's not in the final version.) One of the most disturbing powers, Boehner charged, was that "the health czar will decide which treatment patients could receive and at what cost."

But the section he cited wasn't about allowing some treatments and not others. It was about what benefits your health insurance would *have to* pay for, at a minimum. So, yes, under the new law, the federal government will set a "floor" for how much your health plan has to cover, as we saw in Chapter 2. It *can* cover more, but it has to cover at least that much. If you'd rather pay less for your coverage, and have less protection as a result, you might find these guidelines to be a poor use of government power. But that's not the same thing as the government dictating what treatments you can get.

Overriding the States

Boehner also claimed that "the health choices czar can override state laws regarding covered health benefits. It's in the bill. Go read it." Actually, the bill didn't say anything close to that. The section Boehner cited in his speech said the states can keep requiring health plans to cover more than what the federal government requires. That's important, since many states have lengthy lists of services health insurance has to cover. The only catch was that, if they did, the states had to work out a way to pay back the federal government for subsidizing those extra benefits for low- and middle-income people.

This was how the House tried to preserve the states' laws without spending more of your federal taxes than they absolutely had to. In the end, the law handled the problem in a simpler way. They just won't count the extra state benefits when they figure out how much of a tax credit you'll get to help with your premiums. Of course, this means the federal subsidies might not help you as much if you live in a state with expensive health coverage rules.

Comparative Effectiveness Research

The law doesn't decide how your doctor should take care of you. What it does do is make a big push for "comparative effectiveness research," which is a way of finding out which procedures and treatments work better than others for certain conditions. It sets up a Patient-Centered Outcomes Research Institute, a private, nonprofit outfit that will decide the most important areas that need research, and it provides federal funds to do the research. It will also give funds to the Agency for Healthcare Research and Quality, a federal agency that already works on improving the quality of health care, to train researchers on how to do these kinds of studies and get the results to providers.

For those of us who don't practice medicine, the whole idea of comparative effectiveness research might seem a bit too obvious. Find out what works best? Don't they already do that? Actually, all that the majority of standard medical research does is find out whether a procedure or treatment works better than doing nothing. It doesn't tell you whether one way of treating a disease or injury works better than another way. For that, you need comparative effectiveness research. It has been under way for a while, but it didn't get a lot of funding until 2009, when the stimulus bill provided $1.1 billion over two years to expand the research.

> Comparative effectiveness research looks at different ways of treating the same condition—whether it's two completely different methods, such as drugs versus surgery, or two of the same kinds of treatment, such as one drug versus another.

It's natural, though, to wonder exactly how this research will be used. Congress included a lot of restrictions in the bill to make sure the Department of Health and Human Services wouldn't use the research to deny coverage, or to treat the lives of senior citizens or people with disabilities as any less important than those of healthy people. But the government has to pay some attention to the research results. The Veterans Administration already uses comparative effectiveness research to help guide its health coverage decisions, and the Congressional Budget Office has looked at it as a way to bring overall health care spending down.

Still, the way it usually works is to give doctors a better idea of what might help their patients best. And if the research becomes more widely available, it might be something you can use to learn more about your own treatment options, so you can have a more informed discussion with your doctor about what is likely to work best for you.

The Independent Payment Advisory Board

Sarah Palin singled out this part of the bill, too, calling it "a panel of bureaucrats charged with cutting health care costs on the backs of patients." Actually, it's a presidentially appointed board that will recommend ways to bring down overall Medicare spending. It is supposed to come up with ideas for changing what the program will pay for, if spending keeps rising out of control. But it's not supposed to make decisions for any particular patient. You won't have to check with the Independent Payment Advisory Board to see if you can get that hip replacement.

Still, there's no denying that the board's decisions will carry a lot of power. This is how it will work: Starting in 2014, the fifteen-member board will suggest ways to bring down Medicare spending if it rises beyond certain targets, which are tied to the general rate of inflation. Its suggestions will take effect automatically, unless Congress passes a bill that achieves the same amount of savings in different ways—or unless the Department of Health and Human Services already made spending changes the year before.

And every two years, starting in 2015, the board is supposed to suggest ways to bring down spending throughout the whole health care system. But there are certain things the board won't be able to do. It won't be able to cut your benefits, raise your premiums or your taxes, or change who is eligible for Medicare. So it will have to come up with other ways to bring down spending, such as coordinating people's care better and making medical care more efficient.

The new board will recommend ways to cut Medicare spending, but it won't be able to ration care, cut your benefits, raise your premiums or your taxes, or change who is eligible for Medicare.

There is some real concern about the board. The American Medical Association, which supported the health care bill, opposed the creation of the board because it was worried that the panel would be able to cut physicians' payments. The group also didn't think the board would be flexible enough in looking for expenses to cut, because there might be good reasons for certain kinds of spending to go up. It's hard to know whether these problems are imaginary, or whether they will become real. If they do, it's possible that they could have an indirect impact on your care, if physicians think their services are being cut in the wrong places.

That's something we won't know for a while, and it's worth keeping your eye out for any problems. But this is an issue that's bigger than government making "medical decisions" for you. The real question is, does the government have the right to make broader changes in the kind of health care we'll pay for as a society—especially when it's an actual government health care program such as Medicare? If it doesn't, it's hard to see how we'll ever get runaway health care spending under control. But if it does, it will have to be done in a way that makes smart spending decisions, not sloppy cuts.

Rationing

This is what's really at stake. The oldest scare tactic in the book about health care reform is that it will put the government in charge of rationing our care—telling some people they're not as deserving of health care as other people. And that's what the opponents of the new law claimed, over and over again. But Congress wrote into the law, in as many ways as possible, that these changes cannot be used to ration care. The Independent Payment Advisory Board's Medicare savings ideas, according to the law, "shall not include any recommendation to ration health care." The law also says that the comparative effectiveness research can't be used to steer health care toward healthier people at the expense of those with health problems.

It's reasonable to wonder what the consequences will be when our society tries to control health care spending. But if it's rationed care you're worried about, let's think for a second about what was happening under the old health care system. More than a third of all Americans who tried to buy health insurance on their own either got turned down or got charged too much because of preexisting conditions. And more than one in four Americans, including more than half of those with chronic illnesses, said they went without the health care they needed because it would have cost them too much to pay for it. It was under the old system that we rationed our health care, through private bureaucrats rather than government bureaucrats. And we didn't ration it well, because people who needed care didn't get it.

The challenge is to figure out how to control our health care costs in a smart way, because spending money on everything under the sun doesn't work. We should all keep our guard up to make sure the new system doesn't cut the wrong things. But the old system was cutting the wrong things and hurting people deeply. Now is not the time to wish things could go back to the way they were.

RESOURCES

The **Alliance for Health Reform**, a nonpartisan organization that provides information about health care topics, published a helpful discussion of comparative effectiveness research in August 2008: "Comparative Effectiveness: Better Value for the Money?" It can be found at www .allhealth.org, under "Publications."

The **Henry J. Kaiser Family Foundation** published its own primer on comparative effectiveness research in October 2009, "Explaining Health Reform: What Is Comparative Effectiveness Research?" It can be found at www.healthreform.kff.org.

The **Congressional Budget Office** discussion on how comparative effectiveness research could be used to reduce overall health care spending was published in December 2007. "Research on the Comparative Effectiveness of Medical Treatments: Issues and Options for an Expanded Federal Role" can be found at www.cbo.gov, under "Publications."

The **Center for Healthcare Decisions,** a California-based group that promotes discussions of difficult questions about the trade-offs in health care coverage, has conducted a survey of how people rank their priorities of what needs to be covered and what is less important. The survey, "What Matters Most," can be found at www.sacdecisions.org.

14

How They'll Cut Costs

The biggest challenge in our health care system, other than figuring out how to cover everybody, is figuring out how to get our runaway health care costs under control without hurting your care. The ideal way to do it would be to get rid of only the wasteful spending, so you won't miss it when it's gone. It's going to be hard to hit that target without hitting anything else along the way. But a lot of promising ideas have been emerging in the health care world in recent years. The new law doesn't make a big commitment to any one idea, since we don't know enough yet about what will work best in different parts of the country. Instead, it will test a lot of ideas and see what deserves to be expanded to the rest of the country.

If you're worried about feeling the pinch, it might help to take a look at just how much waste there is in our health care system. We spend more than $2 trillion on health care every year, far more than other developed countries. In fact, we spend about twice as much per person as Canada, Germany, and France and two and a half times as much as the United Kingdom, Italy, and Japan. And as good as our health care is, it's not twice as good as that in these other countries. Some of it is better—the hospitals, the latest drugs and technologies. But we do pretty poorly on measures such as life expectancy and infant mortality.

And health care experts believe that about a third of our spending goes to things that don't make us better. So it's not as if there is no fat to cut. If you thought we were spending all of our health care money wisely, you'd have to explain why Medicare spending in some parts of the country is three times higher than in other places. And according to a Dartmouth study in 2009, about 70 percent of the differences in Medicare spending throughout the country have nothing to do with whether some people are sicker or poorer than others. It's because people in the highest-spending regions are getting more doctor's visits, more days in the hospital, and more high-tech MRI scans and CT scans than people in the rest of the country. The people in the low-spending areas end up just as healthy, and they don't feel they're being short-changed. The people in the high-spending areas are getting more care, but it isn't necessarily better.

In October 2009, the Institute of Medicine estimated that a third of all health care spending in the United States—about $800 billion—goes to medical care that doesn't make us better.

That's especially true when you consider the risks of getting too much care. If you have too many different doctors taking care of you, without talking to one another about what you really need, someone is bound to mess it up. And the more time you spend in a hospital, the more chance there is of something bad happening—such as an infection—so you should go there only when you really, really need to. So, yes, cutting health care spending can hurt you if it's done in the wrong places, and we don't need more managed-care bureaucrats saying no to things we really need. But from what we've learned about the health care system, there is plenty of room to cut back on unnecessary visits and tests, and maybe even make your medical care better by doing it.

In the last chapter, we discussed two of the ways the new law will try to make our health care system less expensive: comparative effectiveness research, to find out more about what works best, and the Independent Payment Advisory Board, to suggest ways to put the brakes on Medicare spending without touching your benefits. But health care experts have identified other approaches as the most promising ideas for fine-tuning your health care, and most of them will get tryouts under the new law. They'll be tested in the Medicare and Medicaid programs, with the idea that if they work well, they can be expanded quickly to save money in the rest of the health care system.

They're complicated, and it's not necessary to know every detail of all of them. You may see one or another of them in your part of the country in the coming years, but probably not all of them. The important thing to know is that they represent different ways of reaching the same goal: paying health care providers not just for giving you a little more of everything, but for working together better so you get the best and most cost-effective care. If these ideas work in the coming years, all of us may be able to pay a bit less for health care without feeling that we're missing anything.

Bundled Payments

Right now, if you go to a hospital, there's not a lot of reason for the hospital to work with the doctor you'll see for follow-up visits after you've been released. The hospital gets paid for its services, your doctor gets paid for her services, and they don't have to talk to each other. No one has to take responsibility for you from beginning to end. The new law will provide money to test a different method, called "bundled payments," which might encourage the two to work together by paying a fixed amount of money that covers all of your care from beginning to end.

Here's how it might work: If you're treated in a hospital, there would be a single payment big enough to cover your hospital care and your follow-up visits to the doctor who will take care of you afterward. That's a big change from the current system, where the more tests you're given, the more money everybody gets. Under a bundled payment system, because they'll have to share the money, the hospital and doctor won't give you one service after another if you don't need it. And it won't be smart for the hospital to ignore you after you've been released. If your doctor doesn't take care of you well—or you're not clear on how to take care of yourself—you'll be back in the hospital, and it will have to spend more money on your care without getting paid more.

So the hospital has more of a reason to check up on you, make sure you really understand your discharge instructions, and coordinate with your doctor to make sure everyone agrees on your follow-up treatment plan. Everyone has more of a reason to avoid expensive mistakes. And everyone has a reason to pay more attention to the costs of their medical devices and supplies, to make sure they're not spending more than they absolutely have to.

Tying together the hospital and follow-up doctor's care is one way to do this. Another way is to set a single payment for chronic conditions, such as diabetes or high blood pressure, where that payment covers all of the care you will need for the entire year.

The new law is going to test bundled payments in the Medicare program. It will be a five-year pilot program to try out the practice among any hospitals, physician groups, home health agencies, and skilled nursing facilities that agree to participate. If it works well, you might see it expanded in 2016. In any experiment like this, of course, there are always possible downsides. For example, it's worth watching to make sure your doctors don't cut corners to save costs. And it's possible that your hospital could try to keep as much money as possible by steering you to a cheap setting for your follow-up care—such as a low-cost nursing facility or rehabilitation center—rather than to the best one for you.

But if bundled payments are handled well, you won't see much difference at all, other than, it is hoped, better follow-up care. And remember, if they cut corners too much and you get sick again, they won't get paid more for the extra medical care you'll need. But they'll still have to treat you. That's a good reason for them to get it right the first time.

Value-Based Payments

Never underestimate the power of rewards. That's another approach the federal government will be testing—this time with Medicare providers throughout the country. Starting in October 2012, hospitals that treat Medicare patients will get part of their payments based on how well they've treated expensive conditions such as heart attacks and pneumonia. And beginning in 2015, Medicare will pay physicians at different rates based on whether they have treated their patients well without wasting money. Over time, the federal government will work up plans to start doing the same thing for skilled nursing facilities and home health agencies.

The idea is to save money for the overall program by paying hospitals and doctors a little bit more to take care of their patients in the best and most cost-effective ways. In both cases, the Department of Health and Human Services will have to figure out how to measure the quality of the care. You might think that these kinds of rewards would cost money, but actually, the Medicare providers are going to have their payments tightened in other ways. For example, their payments will be increased more slowly so providers will be more productive. (See Chapter 9.) They'll have to earn some of that money back, and getting rewards for providing the best care is a good way to do it.

What you'll see depends on how well your doctor or hospital adjusts to the new rules. If you're on Medicare and your doctor or hospital is already using the latest knowledge of what works and what doesn't—or they start focusing more on those kinds of questions—you'll do well. You'll be able to have more confidence that if they order up a new test or procedure for you, it's because you really need it. If your doctor complains a lot about the new rules, and isn't doing well under them, that's a different story. It might be a good time to reconsider whether your doctor is really providing the best care you can get.

There won't always be an easy answer, so don't make a knee-jerk decision to switch to someone else. Maybe your doctor has a good case to make that the new rules are measuring the wrong things. If your doctor is good at a kind of care that isn't being measured, it may make sense to stay with him. If the bad scores on the quality of their care are based on something that's hard to defend—such as ordering too many expensive, high-tech tests—that might be a good reason to start looking around. In any case, it's your cue to start asking questions, because your doctor shouldn't do badly under this kind of system.

And remember, these new rules are going to apply only to Medicare at first, so if you're not on Medicare, you probably won't notice a big difference for a while. But the idea of trying these approaches in Medicare is that they might lead to changes in private insurance down the road, since private insurance often takes its cues from how Medicare pays for things. So if these kinds of payment rewards do well at reducing wasteful health care spending, they might become a more common part of everyone's health care in later years.

Avoiding Problems in Hospitals

We've discussed the rewards. So where are the penalties? You'll find them in another part of the law that tries to crack down on hospital care problems that could have been avoided. Starting in October 2012, hospitals that treat Medicare patients will be paid less if too many of these patients have to be readmitted for complications that we know how to prevent. The new policy will start with awarding the hospitals scores on three serious conditions: heart attacks, heart failure, and pneumonia. Over time, the Department of Health and Human Services can expand the new rule to cover other conditions.

Another part of the law would punish hospitals if their patients got too many "hospital-acquired conditions," such as infections. Starting in October 2014, if a hospital ranks in the top 25 percent of hospitals that have these kinds of problems, it will lose 1 percent of its overall payment from Medicare. Medicare has already stopped paying for several of these conditions by themselves. They're mostly the obvious mistakes—leaving a sponge in a patient after surgery, giving a patient the wrong blood type, or letting a patient get infections of various kinds. But hospitals haven't lost much money on these mistakes, and experts say that policy hasn't been tough enough to make hospitals get more serious about avoiding those kinds of problems.

It's natural to wonder if hospitals that lose payments for these kinds of problems could somehow take it out on you, the patient, by refusing to fix their mistakes. That's not very likely. There are a lot of rules about how hospitals have to treat you if you're having a serious medical problem, so they can't just turn you down. However, there's always the possibility that they could make the rest of us pay in other ways. They could steer patients away who they think are in poor health, and therefore more likely to be readmitted. They could shift the costs of their penalties to patients with private insurance. And a hospital that's already in financial trouble, such as an urban public hospital, might have to close its doors if the penalties make its troubles worse.

There's always the risk that rule changes like these could backfire, and that's why it's important to test them out. See the list of resources at the end of this chapter in case you encounter problems. But it's important for hospitals to face some kind of consequences for making avoidable mistakes, because if they don't, they'll just keep making them. If handled well, these rule changes could give hospitals a strong reason to crack down on mistakes as much as they can.

Medical Homes

It sounds like a simple enough idea: one doctor who looks after us and arranges all of our care, across different settings. Isn't that what health care is supposed to be? But these days it's so hard to find a decent primary care provider, and they're usually so busy, that we don't have anything like that. Instead, we might get to spend a few rushed minutes with a primary care doctor, or we might just go straight to a specialist. If we have a medical problem at night or on a weekend, we're stuck with either an urgent-care clinic or the hospital emergency room. It would be nice to be able to stick with one place, but for most of us, that's not realistic.

That's why the new law is going to encourage experiments with an idea called the "medical home." It's a twist on the old-school idea of the family doctor. A medical team, such as a doctor, nurse, and pharmacist, would handle all of your basic care, get to know you and your needs, and arrange any care you needed from specialists or hospitals. They would make sure the other providers weren't giving you a bunch of tests you'd already had, or medications that would be a bad mix with what you were already taking.

At a medical home, you would have a doctor's office, or possibly a clinic, that you would treat as the "home base" for all of your medical care. If it's run well, it could prevent a lot of the problems that happen when you get bounced around from one medical team to another.

The medical homes would be staffed well enough so that you could actually get an appointment. They'd give you advice on how to stay healthy, and give you a say in all of the decisions about your treatment. You might even be able to communicate with your doctor by email, for a faster response. And the doctor might be able to do something called "e-prescribing"—sending prescriptions directly to a pharmacy electronically, so you don't have the problem of doctor's handwriting that no one can read. If a medical home can coordinate your care better, the theory goes, it will save money in the long run.

The idea is already being tried out in parts of the country, under the Medicare and Medicaid programs and with some private experiments. The new law will try to expand the use of medical homes through the new Center for Medicare and Medicaid Innovation, which is supposed to test the approach, and by providing federal funds to help primary care practices staff up with "community health teams," such as medical specialists, nurses, and pharmacists, so they can become medical homes. If the idea catches on, you might find that one day, your primary care doctor will ask you to sign an agreement stating that her office will become your medical home, and you'll have to tell them if you're going to see a specialist or go to a hospital.

If the medical homes are run well, they might make your life easier in many ways. You'd always have a place to go for medical care, they'd know you, and you could avoid a lot of the problems that can come up when you skip around from place to place for your medical care. There are also ways that they could be run badly, and it's important to know what to watch out for. They could, for example, stand in the way when you're trying to see a specialist, rather than helping you get an appointment. Or they could be paid in a way that rewards them for saying no to care you need, not for coordinating it better.

Those are possibilities that some consumer advocates are warning about, so you should be aware of them. But the advocates are also convinced that medical homes have so much potential to give you better medical care, and allow you to be more involved in it, that they're worth trying more broadly. There are obstacles that could stand in the way— medical practices will have to hire more people to function as medical homes, and they will have to update their technology more than many practices think they can afford. But if they can overcome these obstacles, you may find that medical homes will become a new option for you in the coming years.

Accountable Care Organizations

Another way to get health care providers to work together better is to give them a reason to share responsibility for a patient's care, from beginning to end. "Accountable care organizations" are one way to do that, and they'll get a boost under the new law. With an accountable care association, groups of different kinds of health care providers— such as primary care physicians, specialists, nurse practitioners, and hospitals—agree to take care of their patients across all settings, and get a fixed payment for each patient. If they do this well, and they save money but still score well on all of the quality ratings, they get to keep some of the money they save.

The new law will try to encourage these kinds of groups in the Medicare and Medicaid programs. It will offer to share the Medicare savings with groups that share the responsibility for taking care of people on Medicare, and it will share Medicaid savings with pediatric groups that set themselves up in this way to care for low-income children. Like the other ways of getting providers to save money, there's always the risk that they'll do it in the wrong way. The way the quality of their care is measured will be very important. But if you end up getting your care from one of these organizations, you might find that the different providers work together better.

The key is that they'll have less reason to be turf-conscious and more reason to check in on you wherever you are. If you're in a hospital, under a specialist's care, your primary care doctor might still stop by, and the hospital won't throw him out. In fact, he'll be welcomed, because there's more likely to be a smooth handoff of your care if everyone is involved. And if your care goes smoothly, this will increase the chances that the association will save money—and be able to keep what they save.

Center for Medicare and Medicaid Innovation

This new federal agency, which launches in 2011, will set up a wide range of experiments in the Medicare and Medicaid programs to deliver or pay for health care in new ways. It is supposed to test how medical homes would work for women and for people with chronic conditions. It's also supposed to see what happens when it pays physicians salaries, rather than paying them for each service in different medical settings. It will test ways of providing better coordinated care for people with lots of chronic conditions. And it will try out different ways of paying physicians for advanced diagnostic imaging tests, including paying them more if they follow guidelines and don't overdo it.

It probably sounds like a giant health care laboratory, and in a way, that's what it is. It's supposed to help us learn a lot more than we know now about how to cut health care costs in the right way. If any of these experiments saves money, and provides care that is either as good as or better than the traditional health care settings, the Department of Health and Human Services can expand it and even put it into effect across the country. If not, the experiments end. HHS is supposed to evaluate the tests constantly, and report to Congress once a year on what works and what doesn't.

Medical Lawsuits

There's not a lot in the new law about one idea that's popular with Republicans for controlling health care costs: cutting down on unnecessary medical lawsuits and huge awards for people who win. This is an ongoing argument between the parties in Congress. Most Republicans think you could save a lot of money if doctors didn't feel the need to order so many tests and procedures to cover themselves in case they got sued. A few Democrats agree, but most think there's not much evidence that limits on lawsuits have actually brought down medical costs in the states that have tried them.

The official budget referee, the Congressional Budget Office, disagrees. They think the weight of the evidence suggests that limits on medical lawsuits could save some money—about $11 billion in total health care spending. But that's not actually a huge amount. It's only about a half a percent of what our nation spends every year. The budget office thought the limits could have a bigger impact on the federal deficit, saving $54 billion over ten years. That's because Medicare spends money so much more freely than private insurers.

Still, Democrats didn't see the need to make a big push to control medical lawsuits—especially since the main champions of the idea were Republicans, and they lost their leverage when they fought so hard to kill the bill. Instead, the law will just let the states test alternatives to lawsuits, with a $50 million pot of money to spend on the alternatives over five years. They'll try ideas such as early resolution of disputes before you go to court, but if you're in an area where such an experiment is being tried, you'll be able to opt out of it if you want to preserve your right to sue.

Idea	Effective Date
Alternatives to medical lawsuits	October 1, 2010
Center for Medicare and Medicaid Innovation	January 1, 2011
Medical homes	January 1, 2011
Accountable care organizations	January 1, 2012
Value-based payments	October 1, 2012
Avoiding hospital readmission	October 1, 2012
Bundled payments	January 1, 2013
Avoiding hospital-acquired conditions	October 1, 2014

RESOURCES

Since Medicare will be a testing ground for most of these experiments, **State Health Insurance Counseling and Assistance Programs** (SHIPs) might be able to advise you on what to do if the new approaches are causing trouble for you. They provide one-on-one counseling about what to do in various situations that arise under the Medicare program. You can find the state programs through the Medicare.gov Web site or through the SHIPTalk site, www.shiptalk.org.

The **Medicare Rights Center** hotline is also a good phone number to keep in mind in case you're running into problems. The center is staffed with counselors who can help you or your caregivers with questions about your rights. The number is 1-800-333-4114.

The **National Partnership for Women and Families** has produced several useful, easy-to-read briefs about what medical homes and other experiments might mean to consumers and consumer advocates. You can read their materials on their Web site, www.nationalpartnership .org, by clicking on the "Issues" tab and then "Health Care." Or, if you don't have Internet access, you can call them at (202) 986-2600.

The **Engelberg Center for Health Care Reform,** a project of the Brook-ings Institution, looks closely at the different ideas for bringing costs down and getting better value for the money we spend on health care. Their September 2009 report, "Bending the Curve: Effective Steps to Address Long-Term Health Spending Growth," outlines the views of health care experts across the political spectrum on what ideas are likely to work best. Their Web site is www.brookings.edu/health. You can also order the report by calling Brookings at (202) 797-6000.

The **Foundation for Informed Medical Decision Making,** a Boston-based nonprofit organization, produces "patient decision aids" and research that can help you learn the benefits and risks of different treatment options so you can have a more informed conversation with your doctor. Their Web site is www.informedmedicaldecisions.org, and you can reach them at (617) 367-2000.

15

How They'll Pay for It

You knew this part was coming, so here it is. Someone has to pay for all of the new health care coverage, including the tax credits for people and small businesses and the expansion of Medicaid. You can't just put it on our national credit card. We've got too much stuff on that already. Instead, President Obama told Congress to find ways to pay for the bill, and that's what they did. The bad news is, some of you are going to be stuck with the check.

Not everyone, of course. Congress is smart enough not to charge most of you directly. Some of the money will come from really wealthy people, and if you're doing well enough to be in that category, you can afford it more than the rest of us. (Sorry.) Some of it will come from Medicare providers—assuming they don't lobby Congress to cancel the cuts. And some will come from cutting those extra benefits for Medicare Advantage plans, which you'll miss only if you think the extra frills are the most important things to have.

But some of it will come from the most souped-up health benefit plans. While a lot of those belong to investment bankers and other drowning-in-money types, some of them belong to unions that have settled for better health benefits because their members' companies refused to give raises. Some of the money will come from tax changes that you might not have heard much about, but these could easily affect your pocketbook. And there will be fees and taxes that are supposed to be paid by industry players with lots of money, such as the health insurance companies and the makers of medical devices. There's a risk that they will pass the costs on to you, because that's what they always do, though there will be enough other things happening to lower your premiums that you probably won't feel it.

All of this shows you just how hard it is to find a pain-free way to bring our health care system in line with the rest of the developed world. You can argue with the particular mix that Congress came up with, and in some of these cases, you'd have a lot of company. But nobody gets health care for free, even in the countries that protect their citizens a lot better than we do. The question that Congress struggled with was, should the money come from a narrow group of people, or should be it be spread more broadly? House Democrats wanted it to come mostly from the richest taxpayers, but Senate Democrats, who lean more toward the center than the House, didn't want to pin so many of the costs on the wealthy.

The solution was to spread the costs more broadly. Some of the cost will still be paid by the wealthy, but some of it will come from the most generous health plans, from cutting unnecessary spending in Medicare, from the health care industry, and from changes that could affect middle-class taxpayers. Most of these won't be popular, and there could be surprises along the way that Congress will have to deal with later. But lawmakers hope they can argue that all of the savings will be related to health care, which is where all of the overspending is.

And they can say—in theory, at least—that health care reform will pay for itself. If you were worried that Congress just spent $1 trillion on health care after blowing so much money on Wall Street bailouts, you probably didn't hear that it actually paid for this one. Of course, this means they will have to go through with the various cuts and fees in the bill, and not just cancel them later. If they don't go through with them, or at least find better ways to pay for the changes, then we really are just running up the balance of our national credit card. But the time to worry about that is later, if Congress gets cold feet—not now, when lawmakers have actually taken the risk of paying for what they want to do.

So here is the rundown of the sources of money that Congress has decided to use, and how they're likely to affect you. The vast majority of people will be safe from some of them, but with others, you're likely to pay either directly or indirectly. But remember, the tradeoff for all this is that thirty-two million Americans who didn't have health insurance before might have it now. And even though there's still no complete protection from high medical costs, the rest of you now have a better chance of being safe from financial ruin than you were before. This won't make us the first developed country that protects people from bankruptcy if they get sick. We're just catching up with all the others.

Tax on "Cadillac" Plans

How It Works

It's one thing to give people enough health insurance to help them with their most important health care needs. But when the insurance gets too generous, most health care experts agree, it encourages people to get more health care than they need because they never see any of the bills. This part of the new law would tax the most generous health care plans, widely known as "Cadillac" plans, by charging insurers an excise tax on those plans worth more than $10,200 a year for individual coverage and $27,500 a year for family coverage.

The tax, which doesn't start until 2018, will be on 40 percent of the part of the benefits that are over those limits. And the limits can be raised for health plans that have higher costs than average because of the age and gender of the people in them. A lot of workplaces that have high proportions of older workers or women pay high premiums because their health care costs are expected to be higher than average.

Here's how it might work: You enroll in family health coverage through your workplace that is worth $30,000 a year in benefits. That's $2,500 over the limit. So your health insurer would pay an excise tax on that $2,500. Since the tax is on 40 percent of that amount, the total tax would be $1,000 (and it probably would be passed on to your employer). On the other hand, if you're in a workplace where the age and gender mix raises your limit of acceptable benefits—by, say, $500—then the taxable amount is only $2,000. And since the excise tax is only 40 percent of that amount, the total tax would be $800.

Regular Coverage	Amount
Family benefit limit	$27,500
Family coverage premium	$30,000
Taxable amount	$2,500
Total excise tax	$1,000

Coverage with Age/Gender Adjustment	Amount
Regular family benefit limit	$27,500
With $500 age/gender adjustment	$28,000
Family coverage premium	$30,000
Taxable amount	$2,000
Total excise tax	$800

High-Risk Profession	Amount
Family benefit limit	$27,500
With high-risk adjustment	$30,950
Family coverage premium	$30,000
Taxable amount	$0
Total excise tax	$0

How It Affects You

Most people will never see this tax. For one thing, the average value of health insurance through the workplace is $4,824 for single coverage and $13,375 for family coverage, so the tax will affect only those plans that are far more generous than average. The other reason is that Congress cut this tax way back in the final version of the legislation. When the Senate passed its version of the health care bill, it had planned to tax the benefits starting at lower levels, raising $149 billion over ten years to pay for the expanded health coverage. The final version of the bill would raise $32 billion over ten years—only about 20 percent of the amount in the original version. It also delayed the tax until 2018, which means that many health plans can avoid the tax simply by trimming back benefits before then.

Still, it's not just the Goldman Sachs execs with the gold-plated health care plans who should pay attention to this. It's also union workers, which is one reason why labor unions fought so hard to keep the excise tax completely out of the law—and why House Democrats objected so strongly to it. In recent years, many companies with union members have offered many workers better benefits as a way to avoid raising wages and salaries. So the labor unions argued that the tax would punish them for the concessions they'd already made. Senate Democrats wanted to put the tax in, however, because many economists thought it would be one of the best ways to discourage overspending on health care. The House was able to fight back hard enough to cut the tax to a fraction of what it was. But it's still in the law—in part because Congress needed the money it's supposed to raise.

There are exceptions, however, for people in dangerous jobs. If you're a cop or a firefighter, your health insurance premiums may be high not because your benefits are over the top, but because your job is so risky that you're expensive to insure. So the law raises the limits of nontaxable coverage by an extra $1,650 a year for individuals and an extra $3,450 a year for families. These high-risk professions include:

- Law enforcement officers
- Firefighters
- Emergency medical technicians, paramedics, and first responders
- Longshoremen
- Construction workers
- Miners
- Agricultural workers
- Forestry workers
- Fishing industry workers

The higher limits also apply to early retirees between ages fifty-five and sixty-four, who are receiving retiree health coverage through their former employer and aren't eligible for Medicare yet. And they apply to retirees who worked at least twenty years in a high-risk job.

Another thing to be aware of, however, is that the tax will be calculated using the value of all health benefits you get from your employer, not just health insurance. This can include the reimbursements you get from a health care flexible spending arrangement (FSA) and the contributions your employer makes to your health savings account (HSA). So if, say, you have individual coverage worth $12,000—$1,800 over the limit—and you also have a $2,500 FSA, you will be a total of $3,300 over the limit, and that is the amount that would be taxed.

Over time, the tax could gradually start to reach even more health plans, because more of them will creep up into the range where they are considered "Cadillac" plans. That's because health care costs always increase faster than inflation, so the value of some health care plans will grow so fast they'll be pushed into the taxable range. The law tries to control for this to some extent, by allowing the limits to grow a bit for inflation. In 2019 the limits will increase by the amount of inflation plus 1 percent, but starting in 2020, they will grow only at the rate of inflation, without any extra increase. That won't be enough to keep up with rising medical costs, unless we're controlling costs a lot better than we do now. So you can expect to hear a lot about this issue when that time comes.

Change to the Medical Expenses Deduction

How It Works

Right now, if you pay more than 7.5 percent of your income for medical expenses, you can deduct anything above that level from your taxes. The new law, however, is going to raise that level to 10 percent of your income. So once this part of the law kicks in—in 2013—you'll have to spend a lot more on medical expenses before you can get the deduction. However, that's only true if you're under sixty-five. If you're sixty-five or older, or will turn sixty-five anytime between now and 2016, you get to keep deducting at the 7.5 percent level until 2017.

How It Affects You

This is not a part of the law that got a lot of attention during the debate. The medical expenses deduction is very much a middle-class tax break, because if you earn a lot of money, you're probably not spending enough of your income on medical expenses to make the deduction worth your while. But if you don't earn a lot of money, you usually get a bigger break if you take the standard deduction, rather than itemizing so you can get the break for your medical costs. Even if you are in the middle-income range, you have to spend a lot of money on medical expenses to benefit from the deduction. If you don't, you either won't get the deduction or you won't get very much out of it.

> The medical expenses deduction helps you if you have a lot of expenses that aren't covered by your health insurance. About 12 million people use it, roughly 9 percent of all taxpayers.

You can't use it for over-the-counter medications. Unless it's insulin, you can deduct over-the-counter medication only if a doctor has prescribed it. But you can use the deduction for a wide variety of other expenses—everything from eyeglasses to annual physical exams to acupuncture, and most health insurance premiums, home care, or nursing home care. You can even deduct the cost of an abortion. (Sorry, Congress—you missed that one!)

Congress is counting on this change in the law to raise $15 billion over ten years for the new health care coverage. So why don't senior citizens have to pay? Because senior citizens vote, and the Senate listens to them. Bill Nelson, a Florida Democrat, realized that about half of the people who use the deduction are senior citizens. That's an important tax break for people living on fixed incomes. And when you represent Florida, you pay attention to that kind of thing. So when the Senate Finance Committee was working on its version of the bill, Nelson, who sits on the committee, persuaded his colleague to let seniors keep deducting at the old level of 7.5 percent of their income.

The exemption will last only through the end of 2016, but given how quickly Congress acted to protect senior citizens this time, it shouldn't be too hard to get them to extend it. For everyone else, though, you won't be able to deduct as much as you used to. If this strikes you as unfair, or causes you trouble down the road, the best thing you can do is talk to either the Senate Finance Committee or the House Ways and Means Committee, the two panels that write the tax laws. Their contact information is listed in the resources section at the end of this chapter.

Medicare Provider Payment Cuts

How It Works

The new law will increase Medicare payments to providers more slowly than they would have been increased under the old law, as Congress tries to give them an incentive to be more efficient in how they take care of you. This will apply to such services as inpatient hospital care, home health care, skilled nursing facilities, and hospice care.

How It Affects You

This change is supposed to produce a big chunk of the money for health care reform: $157 billion over ten years. If these cuts actually go through, you might be affected in one of two ways. In theory, the providers could pass the cuts on to you by charging higher rates to anyone with private insurance. Since your health insurance company would be paying more to cover your services, they could charge you higher premiums. But that might not actually happen, because whatever the providers lose from lower than expected Medicare payments, they might earn back by not having so many uninsured people to treat without getting paid for it. The Congressional Budget Office thinks these two trends will more or less cancel each other out.

The other possibility, if you're on Medicare, is that some providers might stop taking Medicare patients because they'd lose too much money. That's the scenario we discussed in Chapter 9. But remember, all of this assumes that Congress won't just back down and repeal the cuts. Here, health care experts disagree on what might happen. The Center on Budget and Policy Priorities, a think tank that focuses on low-income and middle-income people, says Congress has actually let most past Medicare payment cuts stick. But the Congressional Budget Office and the Medicare actuary think that won't happen in this case, because the providers won't become as cost-efficient as Congress wants, and so Congress might have to back down to avoid doing too much damage.

Medicare Advantage Cuts

How It Works

In 2011, payments to Medicare Advantage plans will be frozen at their current level. Then, starting in 2012, the payment formula will start to shift to give more money to low-spending areas and less money to high-spending areas. The plans will also have to give some money back to the government if they spend less than 85 percent of their premiums on health care. If they spend less than 85 percent on health care for three years in a row, they have to stop enrolling new customers. There will be bonus payments to plans that score the best on quality ratings.

How It Affects You

This will also be a major source of funding for health care reform: $136 billion over ten years. As we discussed in Chapter 9, anything that gets cut back in Medicare Advantage plans is likely to be an add-on service, such as vision, hearing, or dental care. It's not going to be the basic services Medicare covers.

You might think this defeats the purpose of getting a Medicare Advantage plan if you lose some of the extra benefits, especially if you've already signed up for one. But it's important to keep this in perspective: It's not the same thing as actually losing your Medicare. Besides, it has become pretty clear that these plans aren't getting you those extra benefits as efficiently as they should. If the lower payments make the plans become more efficient, that might not be the worst thing in the world.

Cuts to Disproportionate Share Hospitals

How It Works

Disproportionate share hospitals are facilities that take care of an unusually large number of low-income patients. (That's why they're called "disproportionate share.") They get extra money from the federal government to make up for all of the uninsured patients they treat. Under the new law, those extra payments will be scaled back, saving $36 billion over ten years.

How It Affects You

It sounds a bit scary at first: cutting payments to important safety-net hospitals at a time when many of them are struggling to survive. But this part of the law was actually designed as part of a deal with hospital industry groups. The trade-off is, since the law is supposed to help uninsured people get health coverage, the hospitals hope they won't have to treat as many uninsured people who can't pay for their care—a change that should cancel out the negative effect of the payment cuts.

The way the new law is written, the payment cuts are supposed to be tied to the actual drop in the number of uninsured people. This may not be a foolproof system, and there's no guarantee that individual hospitals won't still run into trouble. But the hospital industry groups seemed convinced the trade-off will work.

Higher Medicare Premiums

How It Works

If your income is more than $85,000 a year, or if you're a couple who earns more than $170,000 a year, you already have to pay higher premiums for Medicare Part B, which covers physician and outpatient services. Starting in 2011, they're going to stop adjusting those levels for inflation, so more people will have to pay the higher premiums. And if your income is above those same levels, you'll also get less of a subsidy for the premiums for Medicare prescription drug coverage, and you'll have to pay more of it yourself.

How It Affects You

Slightly more than two million senior citizens already earn enough to pay the higher Medicare Part B premiums. Once Medicare stops raising the income limits, more people are going to qualify as high-income earners every year, and so they will slide up into the range where they'll have to pay the extra premiums. If your income is right on the edge of those limits, be prepared for your premiums to be a fair amount higher than you're used to. We won't know the premiums for 2011 and beyond for quite a while, but just to give you an idea, it's not unusual for seniors to pay in the range of $40 a month more once they become classified as "higher income." (The regular premium will be $96.40 a month for most seniors in 2010.)

If you're in that group, the other change you'll see is that you won't get as much of a subsidy for your Medicare prescription drug coverage. Most people on Medicare will pay an average of $30 a month in premiums for their drug coverage. You'll pay a bit more, and we probably won't know how much more until the federal government sets the next round of premiums. But since the drug premiums are so much lower than the Medicare Part B premiums, it's not likely to matter as much.

Higher Medicare Payroll Tax

How It Works

High-income people will have to start paying higher Medicare payroll taxes than everyone else. For individuals who earn more than $200,000 a year and couples who earn more than $250,000 a year, the payroll tax will increase from 1.45 percent of their earnings to 2.35 percent. There will also be a 3.8 percent tax on unearned income—such as earnings from investments—for people in this high-income group.

How It Affects You

This will be a huge source of funding for the reform bill, raising $210 billion over ten years. The changes affect only roughly the top 2 percent of earners, so unless you're in that group, you don't have to worry about this. But it does mean that a small group of wealthy people will be paying for a large share of health care reform for everyone else. This could become a contentious political issue once the higher taxes kick in, in 2013.

If you're in this category, the tax will apply either to your net investment income or to the amount of your modified adjusted gross income that is over the limit—whichever is less. The adjusted gross income thresholds will be $250,000 for a joint return, $125,000 for a married taxpayer filing separately, and $200,000 for anyone else. The kinds of income that will count as net investment income include interest, dividends, annuities, royalties, and rent. For a trade or business, the tax applies to passive activities and the trading of financial instruments or commodities.

More information on this should be available from the IRS eventually. But until then, if you need more technical details, you can look at the explanation put out by the Joint Committee on Taxation, a congressional office that analyzed all of the tax provisions of the new health care law. You can find their Web site at www.jct.gov; see the analysis that came out on March 21, 2010. The publication number is JCX-18-10, and the title is way too long to repeat here. (If you're dying to know, it's mentioned in the Resources section at the end of this chapter.) The section on the unearned income Medicare contribution starts on page 134.

New Savings Account Reimbursement Rules

How It Works

If you have a health savings account (HSA), a health care flexible spending arrangement (FSA), or an Archer medical savings account (MSA), you will be able to pay for medical expenses without being taxed only if they're on the same list that you use for the medical expenses deduction. (See the "Change to the Medical Expenses Deduction" section earlier in this chapter.)

How It Affects You

You will no longer be able to buy over-the-counter medications with these accounts. When you use the medical expenses deduction, you can deduct only medications that were prescribed by a doctor. You can deduct insulin, but nothing else that doesn't have a prescription. Until now, that was not the case with the various kinds of savings accounts. If a doctor told you to take Advil for your headache, you could use your savings in an HSA, an FSA, or an Archer MSA to pay for it without being taxed. But from now on, the Advil won't be a "qualified medical expense" anymore.

> Starting in 2011, you won't be able to use health savings accounts or flexible spending arrangements to pay for over-the-counter medication.

This change in the law is supposed to save $5 billion over ten years. If you want to read up on the new rules, you can find the complete medical deduction expenses list in IRS Publication 502, along with the list of things that don't count. The information on where to find this is listed in the Resources section at the end of this chapter.

Change to Contributions to Flexible Spending Accounts

How It Works

If you want to open a health care FSA at your workplace, starting in 2013, you will be able to put only $2,500 a year into it without paying income or employment taxes.

How It Affects You

Right now the law doesn't set a limit on how much you can contribute to your FSA. It just says your plan has to set some kind of limit—either a dollar amount or a percentage of your income. A lot of people have had higher limits, but now they won't be able to put as much into their accounts. This change is supposed to save $13 billion over ten years, so clearly the government is expecting a lot of people to have to pay taxes who didn't have to pay them before.

Penalties on Health Savings Account Distributions

How It Works

If you have an HSA and you use it to pay for something that isn't a "qualified medical expense," you'll pay a tax penalty of 20 percent, rather than the old penalty of 10 percent. If you have an Archer MSA—the savings account that's aimed at small business workers and the self-employed—your penalty will go up from 15 percent to 20 percent.

How It Affects You

Don't try to pay for that Advil out of your savings account. This rule change isn't a major source of funding for health care reform, compared with some of the others. It's expected to bring in $1.4 billion over ten years, which, by federal standards, is sand off the beach. But since your list of qualified medical expenses is about to change (see the section on "New Savings Account Reimbursement Rules" on page 185), it's a good idea to study the list of "qualified medical expenses" under the medical expenses deduction so you'll know what you can buy and what you can't. It's all in IRS Publication 502, listed in the Resources section at the end of this chapter.

This is also part of a broader pattern in the way the new law treats HSAs. These accounts are favored mostly by Republicans, as a way to get people to cut their health care spending by being more conscious of what everything costs. But the new law was written by Democrats, who never have been wild about HSAs. Their concern is that the accounts are used mostly by people in fairly good health, because if anyone expects to spend a lot on health care, it doesn't make sense to use the accounts. That means the accounts help to create "adverse selection," where healthy people drop out of the more traditional health insurance plans, leaving behind mostly people with more health problems. And those people end up with higher premiums, since it costs the health plans more to take care of them.

The new law doesn't get rid of HSAs. You can still get them if you want them. However, by changing some of the rules about how the accounts are treated—letting you buy fewer things with them, and charging higher penalties if you buy the wrong things—some health care experts believe the law will make HSAs less attractive, so not as many people will get them.

Health Insurance Providers Fee

How It Works

Health insurance companies will have to pay a fee each year, starting in 2014, to help support the expansion of coverage. The thinking in Congress is that, since they stand to gain so much from millions of new customers, they should pick up some of the costs. Nationally, health insurers will have to pay a total of $8 billion in 2014, $11.3 billion each year in 2015 and 2016, $13.9 billion in 2017, and $14.3 billion in 2018. After that, the fees will rise each year to match the increases in premiums. The amount that any one company pays will be based on its share of the market, and the ones with the smallest amount of business will be exempt.

How It Affects You

You're going to pay this fee for the insurance companies, because they're going to charge it to your premiums. However, the good news is that you probably won't feel it, because other things in the new law will lower your premiums enough to cancel out the increase. According to the Congressional Budget Office, the fees would increase premiums slightly if you work for a small business or buy health insurance on your own, and less so if you work for a large company. However, your premiums would also be lowered by reduced administrative costs, so in the end, any impact from the fees shouldn't make a difference. The fees are expected to raise about $60 billion for the health care reform effort over ten years.

Medical Devices Excise Tax

How It Works

The manufacturers, producers, or importers of medical devices will have to pay a 2.3 percent excise tax on the retail price of any taxable device. This won't apply to eyeglasses, contact lenses, or hearing aids, and it probably won't apply to things that are sold over the counter at your local pharmacy for personal use, such as bandages, pregnancy tests, or diabetes testing kits. The Department of Health and Human

Services is expected to put out a list of the common items that would be exempt from the tax.

How It Affects You

This cost could be passed on to you, too, according to the Congressional Budget Office, since it would add to the prices your health insurance would have to pay. But it would raise your premiums by only a small amount, and once again, they would be lowered enough by other factors, such as reduced administrative costs, that you'd never notice it. The excise tax is supposed to raise $20 billion over ten years.

Branded Drugs Fee

How It Works

Companies that manufacture or import brand-name drugs will have to pay an annual fee each year, starting in 2011. Nationally, they will be charged a total of $2.5 billion in 2011, $2.8 billion a year in 2012 and 2013, $3.0 billion a year in 2014 through 2016, $4.0 billion in 2017, $4.1 billion in 2018, and $2.8 billion a year in 2019 and beyond. The fee that any individual company pays will be based on how much it sells to government programs such as Medicare, Medicaid, the Veterans Health Administration, or TRICARE. Companies with the lowest sales will be exempt.

How It Affects You

This fee is the one that's least likely to be passed on to you. Because it doesn't apply to drugs that are sold in the private market, it's not expected to have any real impact on private health insurance premiums. The fee is supposed to raise $27 billion over ten years.

Taxes on Retiree Drug Coverage

How It Works

If employers give prescription drug coverage to their former workers through a retiree health benefits program, they get a federal subsidy that covers about 28 percent of their costs. Until now, they haven't had to pay taxes on that subsidy. Under the new law, they will.

How It Affects You

This subsidy was supposed to encourage employers to keep covering prescription drugs for their retirees, even though there is now a Medicare prescription drug benefit that can cover most of these same people. Now that the subsidies will be taxed, employers won't have as strong a reason to keep paying for your drugs. This change is expected to bring in $4.5 billion over ten years.

So if you get retiree health benefits and they include prescription drug coverage, don't be surprised if your former employer drops the drug coverage. Instead, they might offer to pay your premiums if you switch to the Medicare prescription drug program. They'd save money by doing this, according to the Employee Benefit Research Institute, which studies private-sector benefit trends. So you wouldn't necessarily lose your prescription drug benefit. It would just shift to another source. You'll have to hope Medicare closes its "donut hole" quickly, though, so you don't have to deal with that unfortunate gap in drug coverage.

Change	Effective Date
Medicare provider payment cuts	Varies by provider, starting in 2010
Medicare Advantage cuts	January 1, 2011
Higher Medicare premiums	January 1, 2011
New health savings account reimbursement rules	January 1, 2011
Penalties on health savings account distributions	January 1, 2011
Branded drugs fee	January 1, 2011
Changes to medical expenses deduction:	
• For taxpayers under sixty-five	January 1, 2013
• For taxpayers sixty-five or older	January 1, 2017*
Changes to contributions to flexible spending accounts	January 1, 2013
Higher Medicare payroll tax	January 1, 2013
Medicare tax on unearned income	January 1, 2013
Taxes on retiree drug coverage	January 1, 2013
Medical devices excise tax	January 1, 2013
Cuts to disproportionate share hospitals	October 1, 2013 (fiscal year 2014)
Health insurance providers fee	January 1, 2014
Tax on "Cadillac" plans	January 1, 2018

---

*The delay applies to anyone who turns sixty-five in 2013, 2014, 2015, or 2016.

RESOURCES

If you need more technical details on the tax changes, your best bet—until the IRS puts out its own guidance—is to look at the analysis of the new law by the **Joint Committee on Taxation,** a congressional office that studies the impact of everything Congress does to the tax code. It's not literature. It's as technical as you can possibly get. But for now it will give you the details you need if you think you might be affected and need to learn more about the new tax rules. (Seriously, it's really technical.)

To find it, go to their Web site, www.jct.gov, and look it up by its publication number, JCX-18-10. It came out on March 21, 2010. At the risk of scaring or boring you, the title is, "Technical Explanation of the Revenue Provisions of the 'Reconciliation Act of 2010,' As Amended, In Combination with the 'Patient Protection and Affordable Care Act.'"

You can find out all about the medical expenses deduction by looking at **IRS Publication 502,** which explains how the deduction works and has the complete list of what you can and can't deduct. It's available online at www.irs.gov/publications/p502, or you can order it by calling 1-800-829-1040.

The **Senate Finance Committee** is one of the two committees that writes the tax laws, and it's one of two Senate panels that handle health care issues. If you're facing problems because of these tax changes, you can call the committee at (202) 224-4515, or write to them at 219 Dirksen Senate Office Building, Washington, DC 20510-6200. The Web site is www.finance.senate.gov.

The **House Ways and Means Committee** is the other committee that writes the tax laws, and it's one of the three House panels that worked on the health care bill. If the tax changes cause problems for you and you want to let them know about it, you can call them at (202) 225-3625, or write to them at 1102 Longworth House Office Building, Washington, DC 20515. If you don't mind submitting comments electronically, you can do it through the committee's Web site, www.waysandmeans .house.gov.

Appendix

State Insurance Agencies

These are the agencies that regulate insurance in your state, including private health insurance, and should be able to help you apply for coverage and deal with problems. In some cases, these are main phone numbers, and it may take you a few more steps to find the exact office. Whenever possible, the phone numbers go directly to the consumer affairs office or a similar division that's designed to help with your needs.

Alabama Department of Insurance
201 Monroe Street
Suite 1700
Montgomery, AL 36104
(334) 269-3550
www.healthinsurance.alabama.gov

Alaska Division of Insurance
State Office Building, 9th floor
333 Willoughby Avenue 99801
Juneau, AK 99811
(800) 467-8725
www.commerce.state.ak.us/insurance

Arizona Department of Insurance
2910 N 44th Street, Suite 210 (2nd floor)
Phoenix, AZ 85018
(602) 364-2499
www.id.state.az.us

Arkansas Insurance Department
Life and Health Division
1200 West Third Street
Little Rock, AR 72201
(501) 371-2600
www.insurance.arkansas.gov

California Department of Insurance
Consumer Services Division
300 South Spring Street, South Tower
Los Angeles, CA 90013
(800) 927-4357
www.insurance.ca.gov

Colorado Division of Insurance
1560 Broadway, Suite 850
Denver, CO 80202
(303) 894-7490
www.dora.state.co.us/insurance

Connecticut Insurance Department
Consumer Affairs Unit
PO Box 816
Hartford, CT 06142
(800) 203-3447
www.ct.gov/cid

Delaware Insurance Department
841 Silver Lake Boulevard
Dover, DE 19904
(800) 282-8611
www.delawareinsurance.gov

**District of Columbia Department of Insurance,
    Securities and Banking**
810 First Street NE, Suite 701
Washington, DC 20002
(202) 727-8000
www.disr.dc.gov/disr

Florida Office of Insurance Regulation
200 East Gaines Street
Tallahassee, FL 32399
(850) 413-3140
www.floir.com

Georgia Office of Insurance and Safety Fire Commissioner
Life and Health Division
2 Martin Luther King, Jr. Drive
West Tower, Suite 704
Atlanta, GA 30334
(404) 656-2085
www.gainsurance.org

Hawaii Department of Commerce and Consumer Affairs
Insurance Division
King Kalakaua Building
335 Merchant Street, Room 213
Honolulu, HI 96813
(808) 586-2790
www.hawaii.gov/dcca/ins

Idaho Department of Insurance
700 West State Street
PO Box 83720
Boise, ID 83720
(800) 721-3272
www.doi.idaho.gov

Illinois Department of Insurance
320 W Washington Street
Springfield, IL 62767
(877) 527-9431
www.insurance.illinois.gov

Indiana Department of Insurance
Consumer Services Division
311 W Washington Street, Suite 300
Indianapolis, IN 46204
(317) 232-2385
www.in.gov/idoi

Iowa Insurance Division
330 Maple Street
Des Moines, IA 50319
(877) 955-1212
www.iid.state.ia.us

Kansas Insurance Department
420 SW 9th Street
Topeka, KS 66612
(800) 432-2484
www.ksinsurance.org

Kentucky Department of Insurance
215 W Main Street
Frankfort, KY 40601
(800) 595-6053
www.insurance.ky.gov/kentucky

Louisiana Department of Insurance
1702 N 3rd Street
Baton Rouge, LA 70802
(800) 259-5300
www.ldi.la.gov

**Maine Department of Professional and
    Financial Regulation**
Bureau of Insurance
76 Northern Avenue
Gardiner, ME 04345
(800) 300-5000
www.maine.gov/pfr/insurance

Maryland Insurance Administration
200 St. Paul Place, Suite 2700
Baltimore, MD 21202
(800) 492-6116
www.mdinsurance.state.md.us

**Massachusetts Office of Consumer Affairs
and Business Regulation**
Division of Insurance
One South Station, 5th floor
Boston, MA 02110
(617) 521-7794
www.mass.gov/doi

**Michigan Department of Energy, Labor
and Economic Growth**
Office of Financial and Insurance Regulation
611 West Ottawa Street, 3rd floor
Lansing, MI 48933
(877) 999-6442
www.michigan.gov/dleg

Minnesota Department of Commerce
Office of the Insurance Commissioner
85 7th Place East, Suite 500
St. Paul, MN 55101
(651) 296-2488
www.insurance.mn.gov

Mississippi Insurance Department
1001 Woolfolk State Office Building
501 N West Street
Jackson, MS 39201
(800) 562-2957
www.mid.state.ms.us

Missouri Department of Insurance, Financial Institutions and Professional Registration
Consumer Affairs Division
301 West High Street, Room 530
Jefferson City, MO 65101
(800) 726-7390
www.insurance.mo.gov

Montana Commissioner of Securities and Insurance
840 Helena Avenue
Helena, MT 59601
(800) 332-6148
www.sao.state.mt.us

Nebraska Department of Insurance
Terminal Building
941 O Street, Suite 400
Lincoln, NE 68508
(877) 564-7323
www.doi.ne.gov

Nevada Division of Insurance
788 Fairview Drive, Suite 300
Carson City, NV 89701
(775) 687-4270
www.doi.state.nv.us

New Hampshire Insurance Department
21 South Fruit Street, Suite 14
Concord, NH 03301
(800) 852-3416
www.nh.gov/insurance

New Jersey Department of Banking and Insurance
20 West State Street
Trenton, NJ 08625
(800) 446-7467
www.state.nj.us/dobi

New Mexico Public Regulation Commission
Insurance Division
P.E.R.A. Building
1120 Paseo De Peralta
Santa Fe, NM 87501
(888) 427-5772
www.nmprc.state.nm.us

New York State Insurance Department
Health Bureau
1 Commerce Plaza
Albany, NY 12257
(518) 474-6272
www.ins.state.ny.us

North Carolina Department of Insurance
Dobbs Building
430 N Salisbury Street
Raleigh, NC 27603-5926
(800) 546-5664
www.ncdoi.com

North Dakota Insurance Department
State Capitol, 5th floor
600 E Boulevard Avenue
Bismarck, ND 58505-0320
(800) 247-0560
www.nd.gov/ndins

Ohio Department of Insurance
50 W Town Street, 3rd floor, Suite 300
Columbus, OH 43215
(800) 686-1526
www.insurance.ohio.gov

Oklahoma Insurance Department
2401 NW 23rd Street, Suite 28
Oklahoma City, OK 73107
(800) 522-0071
www.ok.gov/oid

Oregon Department of Consumer and Business Services
Insurance Division
350 Winter Street NE
Salem, OR 97301
(888) 877-4894
www.cbs.state.or.us/external/ins

Pennsylvania Insurance Department
1326 Strawberry Square
Harrisburg, PA 17120
(877) 881-6388
www.insurance.pa.gov

Rhode Island Department of Business Regulation
Office of the Health Insurance Commissioner
1511 Pontiac Avenue
Building No. 69, 1st floor
Cranston, RI 02920
(401) 462-9517
www.ohic.ri.gov

South Carolina Department of Insurance
1201 Main Street, Suite 1000
Columbia, SC 29201
(803) 737-6160
www.doi.sc.gov

South Dakota Division of Insurance
445 East Capitol Avenue
Pierre, SD 57501
(605) 773-3563
www.state.sd.us/drr2/reg/insurance

Tennessee Department of Commerce and Insurance
Insurance Division
500 James Robertson Parkway
Nashville, TN 37243
(615) 741-2176
www.state.tn.us/commerce/insurance

Texas Department of Insurance
333 Guadalupe Street
Austin, TX 78701
(800) 252-3439
www.tdi.state.tx.us

Utah Insurance Department
State Office Building, Room 3110
Salt Lake City, UT 84114
(800) 439-3805
www.insurance.utah.gov

Vermont Department of Banking, Insurance, Securities and Health Care Administration
Division of Health Care Administration
89 Main Street
Montpelier, VT 05620
(800) 631-7788
www.bishca.state.vt.us/HcaDiv

Virginia State Corporation Commission
Bureau of Insurance
Tyler Building
1300 E Main Street
Richmond, VA 23219
(800) 552-7945
www.scc.virginia.gov/division/boi

West Virginia Offices of the Insurance Commissioner
Consumer Service Division
1124 Smith Street, Room 309
Charleston, WV 25301
(888) 879-9842
www.wvinsurance.gov

Washington State Office of the Insurance Commissioner
5000 Capitol Boulevard
Tumwater, WA 98501
(800) 562-6900
www.insurance.wa.gov

Wisconsin Office of the Commissioner of Insurance
125 South Webster Street
Madison, WI 53703
(800) 236-8517
www.oci.wi.gov

Wyoming Insurance Department
106 East 6th Avenue
Cheyenne, WY 82002
(800) 438-5768
www.insurance.state.wy.us

State Medicaid Offices

These are the departments and agencies that oversee the Medicaid program. When possible, this list identifies the phone numbers and Web sites that should be able to help you apply directly for Medicaid coverage. Where these are not available, they will help you find the regional office in your area where you can sign up. Some of these agencies can also help you apply for the State Children's Health Insurance Program or direct you to the right office.

Alabama Medicaid Agency
501 Dexter Avenue
Montgomery, AL 36104
(800) 362-1504
www.medicaid.alabama.gov

Alaska Department of Health and Social Services
350 Main Street, Room 404
Juneau, AK 99811
(907) 465-3030
www.hss.state.ak.us/dpa

Arizona Health Care Cost Containment System
801 E Jefferson Street
Phoenix, AZ 85034
(877) 764-5437
www.azahcccs.gov

Arkansas Department of Human Services
Donaghey Plaza South, Slot S201
PO Box 1437
Little Rock, AR 72203
(800) 482-8988
www.arkansas.gov/dhs

California Department of Health Care Services
Medi-Cal Eligibility
PO Box 997417, MS 4607
Sacramento, CA 95899
(916) 552-9200
www.medi-cal.ca.gov

Colorado Department of Health Care Policy and Financing
1570 Grant Street
Denver, CO 80203
(303) 866-2993
www.chcpf.state.co.us

Connecticut Department of Social Services
25 Sigourney Street
Hartford, CT 06106
(800) 842-1508
www.dss.state.ct.us

Delaware Department of Health and Social Services
Division of Medicaid and Medical Assistance
1901 N Du Pont Highway, Lewis Building
New Castle, DE 19720
(302) 255-9500
www.dhss.delaware.gov/dhss/dmma

District of Columbia Department of Health Care Finance
825 North Capitol Street, NE, Suite 500
Washington, DC 20001
(202) 442-5988
www.dhcf.dc.gov

Florida Agency for Health Care Administration
2727 Mahan Drive
Tallahassee, FL 32308
(888) 419-3456
www.fdhc.state.fl.us

Georgia Department of Community Health
2 Peachtree Street, NW
Atlanta, GA 30303
(404) 656-4507
www.dch.georgia.gov

Hawaii Department of Human Services
Med-QUEST Division
1390 Miller Street, Room 209
Honolulu, HI 96813
(800) 316-8005
www.med-quest.us

Idaho Department of Health and Welfare
PO Box 83720
Boise, ID 83720
(800) 926-2588
www.healthandwelfare.idaho.gov

Illinois Department of Healthcare and Family Services
201 South Grand Avenue, East
Springfield, IL 62763
(800) 226-0768
www.hfs.illinois.gov

Indiana Families and Social Services Administration
402 West Washington Street
Indianapolis, IN 46204
(317) 233-4454
www.in.gov/fssa

Iowa Department of Human Services
Hoover State Office Building
1305 E Walnut Street
Des Moines, IA 50319
(800) 972-2017
www.dhs.state.ia.us

Kansas Department of Social and Rehabilitation Services
915 SW Harrison Street
Topeka, KS 66612
(800) 792-4884
www.srskansas.org/hcp

Kentucky Cabinet for Health and Family Services
275 E Main Street
Frankfort, KY 40621
(800) 635-2570
www.chfs.ky.gov

Louisiana Department of Health and Hospitals
628 N 4th Street
Baton Rouge, LA 70802
(225) 342-9500
www.dhh.louisiana.gov

Maine Department of Health and Human Services
Office of MaineCare Services
11 State House Station
Augusta, ME 04333
(800) 321-5557
www.maine.gov/dhhs/oms

Maryland Department of Health and Mental Hygiene
201 West Preston Street
Baltimore, MD 21201
(877) 463-3464
www.dhmh.state.md.us

Massachusetts Office of Health and Human Services
MassHealth program
1 Ashburton Place, 11th floor
Boston, MA 02108
(888) 665-9993
www.mass.gov/masshealth

Michigan Department of Community Health
Capitol View Building
201 Townsend Street
Lansing, MI 48913
(517) 373-3740
www.michigan.gov/mdch

Minnesota Department of Human Services
PO Box 64838
St. Paul, MN 55164
(800) 657-3739
www.dhs.state.mn.us

Mississippi Division of Medicaid
Sillers Building
550 High Street, Suite 1000
Jackson, MS 39201
(800) 421-2408
www.medicaid.ms.gov

Missouri Department of Social Services
HealthNet Division
615 Howerton Court
PO Box 6500
Jefferson City, MO 65102
(888) 275-5908
www.dss.mo.gov/mhd/index.htm

Montana Department of Public Health and Human Services
111 North Sanders, Room 301
Helena, MT 59620
(800) 332-2272
www.dphhs.mt.gov/programsservices/medicaid.shtml

Nebraska Department of Health and Human Services
301 Centennial Mall South
Lincoln, NE 68509
(402) 471-3121
www.accessnebraska.ne.gov

Nevada Department of Health and Human Services
Division of Welfare and Supportive Services
1470 College Parkway
Carson City, NV 89706
(800) 992-0900
www.dwss.nv.gov

New Hampshire Department of Health and Human Services
97 Pleasant Street
Concord, NH 03301
(800) 852-3345, ext. 5254
www.dhhs.state.nh.us/DHHS/MEDICAIDPROGRAM

New Jersey Department of Human Services
Division of Medical Assistance and Health Services
PO Box 712
Trenton, NJ 08625
(800) 356-1561
www.state.nj.us/humanservices/dmahs

New Mexico Human Services Department
Medical Assistance Division
2009 S Pacheco, Pollon Plaza
Santa Fe, NM 87504
(888) 997-2583
www.hsd.state.nm.us/mad

New York State Department of Health
Corning Tower
Empire State Plaza
Albany, NY 12237
(800) 541-2831
www.health.state.ny.us/health_care/medicaid

North Carolina Department of Health and Human Services
Division of Medical Assistance
1985 Umstead Drive
Raleigh, NC 27603
(800) 662-7030
www.dhhs.state.nc.us/dma/medicaid

North Dakota Department of Human Services
Medical Services
600 East Boulevard Avenue, Dept. 325
Bismarck, ND 58505
(877) 543-7669
www.nd.gov/dhs/services/medicalserv

Ohio Department of Job and Family Services
Office of Ohio Health Plans
50 West Town Street
Columbus, OH 43215
(800) 324-8680
www.jfs.ohio.gov/ohp

Oklahoma Health Care Authority
4545 N Lincoln Boulevard, Suite 124
Oklahoma City, OK 73105
(800) 522-0310
www.okhca.org

Oregon Health Plan
Division of Medical Assistance Programs
Administrative Office
500 Summer Street, NE
Salem, OR 97301
(800) 359-9517
www.oregon.gov/DHS/healthplan

Pennsylvania Department of Public Welfare
Office of Medical Assistance Programs
Health and Welfare Building, Room 515
PO Box 2675
Harrisburg, PA 17105
(717) 787-1870
www.humanservices.state.pa.us/compass

Rhode Island Department of Human Services
Louis Pasteur Building
600 New London Avenue
Cranston, RI 02921
(401) 462-5300
www.dhs.ri.gov

South Carolina Department of Health
   and Human Services
PO Box 8206
Columbia, SC 29202
(888) 549-0820
www.dhhs.state.sc.us

South Dakota Department of Social Services
700 Governors Drive
Pierre, SD 57501
(605) 773-4678
www.dss.sd.gov/medicaleligibility

TennCare
310 Great Circle Road
Nashville, TN 37243
(866) 311-4287
www.state.tn.us/tenncare

Texas Health and Human Services Commission
Brown-Heatly Building
4900 N Lamar Boulevard
Austin, TX 78751
(877) 541-7905 (or dial 2-1-1)
www.hhsc.state.tx.us

Utah Department of Health
Division of Medicaid and Health Financing
PO Box 143106
Salt Lake City, UT 84114
(800) 662-9651
www.health.utah.gov/medicaid

Office of Vermont Health Access
312 Hurricane Lane, Suite 201
Williston, VT 05495
(800) 250-8427
www.ovha.vermont.gov

Virginia Department of Medical Assistance Services
600 East Broad Street
Richmond, VA 23219
(804) 786-6145
www.dmas.virginia.gov

Washington State Department of Social and Health Services
Health and Recovery Services Administration
Customer Service Center
PO Box 45505
Olympia, WA 98504
(800) 562-3022
www.hrsa.dshs.wa.gov/HRSAClient.htm

West Virginia Department of Health and Human Resources
Bureau for Medical Services
350 Capitol Street, Room 251
Charleston, WV 25301
(800) 642-8589
www.wvdhhr.org/bms

Wisconsin Department of Health Services
1 West Wilson Street
Madison, WI 53703
(800) 362-3002
www.access.wisconsin.gov

Wyoming Department of Health
Office of Healthcare Financing
6101 Yellowstone Road, Suite 210
Cheyenne, WY 82002
(307) 777-7531
www.health.wyo.gov/healthcarefin/equalitycare

Acknowledgments

This book was possible only because of the people who took a chance on a first-time author, and the many people who answered my annoying questions even when they had other things to do.

Special thanks to Senator Tom Daschle for suggesting me for the project, back when St. Martin's Press was looking for someone to take it on. There were many talented people who could have done this, and it was an honor to have the chance. Victoria Skurnick at Levine Greenberg was a patient agent who talked me through the mysteries of book contracts and helped me figure out the best strategies for knocking this out fast.

At St. Martin's Press, Tom Dunne was generous enough to let me do this without the full book proposal treatment. I'll always be grateful for his confidence, and his lack of stress when the health care bill almost died. Karyn Marcus was as encouraging as any book editor could be, and knows just what to say to get the best out of her writers: "This looks great. Can you finish it faster?"

Bill Vaughan, formerly of Consumers Union and the House Ways and Means Committee, passed on lots of useful guidance for consumers and great suggestions on the book outline and one of the early chapters. Mark McClellan of the Engelberg Center for Health Care Reform provided helpful feedback on the book outline and a skeptical, and wise, perspective on the long-term costs of the new system.

The staff of the Senate Finance Committee were kind enough to answer my picky policy questions even as they were trying to recover from the end of the health care debate. Thanks also to Rima Cohen and Nick Papas at the Department of Health and Human Services, who took time from their busy schedules to help me with some last-minute clarity.

At the Center on Budget and Policy Priorities, January Angeles checked my math and suggested some good additions to the table on health care tax credits and subsidies in Chapter 4.

Bruce Lesley of First Focus, Tricia Brooks of the Georgetown University Center for Children and Families, and Steve Hitov of the National Health Law Program all provided valuable information on the future of the State Children's Health Insurance Program and resources for people who need help in the Medicaid program.

A big shout-out goes to Anne Montgomery of the Senate Special Committee on Aging, who patiently explained the nuts and bolts of the long-term care section that no one hears enough about, including the CLASS Act and the new nursing home rules.

Len Nichols of the New America Foundation talked me through some of the cost-cutting experiments in Chapter 14 that are the hardest for normal people to understand. Sabrina Corlette of the National Partnership for Women & Families suggested some helpful, consumer-friendly ways of looking at the new methods of delivering health care, particularly medical homes.

If this book helps you make sense of the new health care system, it will only be because the gang at Congressional Quarterly, and at the Bureau of National Affairs before that, gave me a front-row seat for so many years to learn about health care and Congress in general. Both are news organizations that do exactly what the public says it wants the mainstream media to do. They focus on substance, every day, and they do it well. Thanks to both for giving me the background that made this book possible.

Thanks, of course, to Mom, Dad, Wendy and her gang, and Lara for the unconditional love and support for so many years. And to my wonderful parents-in-law, Bernie and Judy Leif, for all of the encouragement and the helpful updates on health care news.

Most of all, thanks to Elissa for being so awesome. And to Jessa and Gabe, for amazing me every single day—and for letting me use the computer sometimes.

Index

abortion, 80–81
accountable care organization, 167–68
actuarial value, 77
Administration on Aging, 21
adverse selection, 8, 188
Advisory Committee on Immunization Practices, 126, 147–48
Aetna, 16
Agency for Healthcare Research and Quality, 147, 152–54
Alliance for Health Reform, 156–57
American Medical Association, 155
annual limits, 28, 31–32, 96, 102
appeals, 17–21, 23, 30–31, 79, 100–104, 117
Arizona, 18–19, 127

bankruptcy, 4, 15, 25, 174
Blue Cross, 28, 90–91
Boehner, John, 151–52
branded drugs fee, 190–91, 192

breast cancer, 15, 112, 142, 144
Bright Futures, 148
bronze-level plans, 16, 29, 30, 76

"Cadillac" Plans, 174–78, 192
California, 15, 18–19, 22, 28, 68
Georgetown University Health Policy Institute report, 24
Canada, 88, 112, 158
catastrophic plan, 13, 30, 36, 76–77
Center for American Progress Action Fund, 15, 38
Center for Healthcare Decisions, 157
Center for Medicare Advocacy, 118
Center on Budget and Policy Priorities, 77
Centers for Disease Control and Prevention, 21, 144, 147
children, 36, 128
Medicaid for, 120, 124
pediatric services, 29, 124, 148, 168
preexisting conditions, 97

children (*continued*)
State Children's Health Insurance
Program, 7, 35, 38, 42, 47, 59, 68,
99, 106, 107, 122–24, 126–27
young adults on parents' plan, 98,
103–4
Children's Defense Fund, 68
Children's Health Insurance Program,
7, 35, 38, 47, 68, 126–27
health insurance exchanges
impacting, 85–86
new rules effective date, 123
quick changes impacting, 107
subsidies v., 59
chronic disease management, 29
claim, 19
CLASS Act, 131–34
Clinton, Bill, 62, 150
COBRA Continuation Health
Coverage, 16–17
coinsurance, 19
community health center, 129
Community Living Assistance
Services and Supports Act
(CLASS Act), 131–34
comparative effectiveness research,
152–57, 160
complaints, 57, 79, 101, 136
Patient Advocate Foundation,
18–19
confusion, about new law, 3
Congressional Budget Office,
3, 27–28, 73, 89–91, 157
on co-op idea, 92
on Medicare providers, 115
on small businesses, 66
Connecticut, 18–19
Conrad, Kent, 91–92
consumer groups, 13–14, 22–23, 24
Consumer Operated and Oriented
Plan (CO-OP), 91–92
Co-ops, 91–92, 94
copayments, 11–14, 20, 41, 47, 78,
125
toward out-of-pocket expenses,
15–16
"Cornhusker Kickback," 123

cost, for new program, 172–74
branded drugs fee, 190–91
changes/effective dates, 192
contributions to FSAs, 186–87
disproportionate share hospitals,
182–83
health insurance providers fee,
188–89
higher Medicare payroll tax,
184–85, 192
higher Medicare premiums, 183–84
medical devices excise tax, 189–90,
192
medical expenses deduction,
178–80
Medicare Advantage cuts, 181–82,
192
penalties on HSAs, 187–88
savings account reimbursement
rules, 185–86
tax on "Cadillac" Plans, 174–78,
192
taxes on retiree drug coverage,
191, 192
Cover Florida Health Care Access
Program, 12–13
coverage, 2
canceled for sick people, 2, 9,
27–28, 31, 34, 45, 96–97, 102
commonalties in, 7–8
ease of signing up, 64
exemptions, 37, 39–40, 42–43,
72, 75
expensive, 63–64, 174–75
types of, 7

death panels, 150–51
death spirals, 8–11
deductible, 10–14, 19–20, 41, 77–79,
83, 109–10, 112, 125
Democrats. *See also specific person*
on abortion, 80–81
co-op idea, 91–92
dispute over cheaper coverage,
93–94
on public option goals, 89–90
on subsidies v. income levels, 52

dental care, 114, 124–25, 182
Department of Health and Human
    Services (DHS), 5, 20–21, 45–46,
    73, 78, 127, 153
  announcement of first open
    enrollment, 86
  health plan options, 99–100
  how subsidies work, 53
  separate funds for abortion, 81
  temporary risk pools, 97–98
Department of Labor, 19, 21
DHS. *See* Department of Health and
    Human Services
disabilities, persons with, 19, 26,
    119, 121–22, 131, 138, 150–51,
    153
  Medicaid, 120
  Medicare, 7
doctor visits
  Medicaid's benefits covering, 124
  trouble finding doctors, 125–26
donut holes, 102–3, 106, 108–12,
    117, 191

Early and Periodic Screening,
    Diagnosis, and Treatment
    (EPSDT), 124
ehealthinsurance.com, 22
  time limit for uninsured, 45–46
Eldercare Locator, 140
elderly. *See* seniors
emergencies, 12, 13, 29, 30, 36, 76
Employee Benefit Research Institute,
    69
Employee Benefits Security
    Administration, 19, 21
Employee Retirement Income
    Security Act (ERISA), 19, 21
employers
  fined for not covering employees,
    62
  required to give information, 65
  shared responsibility of, 61
end-of-life care, 140, 150
Engelberg Center for Health Care
    Reform, 171
Ensign, John, 40

EPSDT. *See* Early and Periodic
    Screening, Diagnosis, and
    Treatment
ERISA. *See* Employee Retirement
    Income Security Act
"evidence of coverage," 16, 18, 100
exclusions, 20
exemptions, 37, 39–40, 42–43, 72, 75
external review, 18–20, 30

Families USA, 22–23
family planning, Medicaid covering,
    124
Federal Administration on Aging,
    140
Federal Employees Health Benefits
    Program, 74, 90–91
fee-for-service system, 10, 113
Fifth Amendment, 40
First Focus, 68
Flexible Spending Account (FSA),
    177, 185–87
Florida, 12–13, 18–19
Food and Drug Administration, 21
Foundation for Informed Medical
    Decision Making, 171
France, 158
"free choice vouchers," 64–65

Georgetown University Health Policy
    Institute, 15, 24
Germany, 9, 158
gold-level plans, 16, 29, 58, 72, 76
Group Health Cooperative of Puget
    Sound, 92
guaranteed issue and renewal, 31–32

Hacker, Jacob, 87–88
Hawaii, 18–19
Health Care Choice Compacts, 93, 94
"Health Connector," 2, 15–16, 24,
    38–39, 72–73, 82
health insurance exchanges, 2, 26,
    69, 85. *See also* State Children's
    Health Insurance Program
  abortion coverage availability, 79–81
  benefits of state-based, 15–16

health insurance exchanges *(continued)*
    better information on plan options,
        78–79, 99–100
    children's benefits, 127
    eligibility for, 74
    employers required to inform
        about, 65
    how subsidies work, 53
    illegal immigrants, 81–82
    individual health insurance,
        2, 15–16, 84
    Massachusetts example, 82
    Medicare, 85
    medium/large business, 66–67, 74,
        83–84
    ombudsman offices availability, 79
    small business, 2, 15–16, 66, 74, 83
    splitting the difference between
        private and public option,
        90–91
    types of plans offered, 76–78
    uninsured people, 84–85
    as virtual marketplaces, 71, 74–76
health insurance providers fee,
    188–89, 192
Health Maintenance Organization
    (HMO), 10, 113
Health Savings Account (HSA),
    10–11, 187–88
Henry J. Kaiser Family Foundation,
    3, 66–67, 109–10, 117, 157
HMO. *See* Health Maintenance
    Organization
home health care, 124, 180
honesty
    about subsidy need, 54
    Aetna Advantage Plan, 16
    nursing facilities', 136
hospital services, 13, 14, 29, 124,
    164–65
    cuts to disproportionate share,
        182–83, 192
House Energy and Commerce
    Committee, 113
House Ways and Means Committee,
    193–94
HSA. *See* Health Savings Account

illegal immigrants, 81–82, 128
Illinois, 18–19
income percentage, penalties v., 42
Independent Payment Advisory
    Board's Medicare, 154, 156
Indian Health Service, 21
individual health insurance, 2, 4
    Georgetown University Health
        Policy Institute guides/reports,
        24
    health insurance exchanges, 2,
        15–16, 84
    if you currently have, 58
    new rules, 34, 44–45, 67
    quick changes for, 104–5
    tax credit/effective date, 56
individual mandate, 37–40
insurekidsnow.gov, 128
Internal Revenue Service
    penalties for not enrolling, 41–43
    Publication 502, 185, 186,
        188, 193
internal review, 20

Joint Committee on Taxation, 193

laboratory services, 29, 124
large companies
    health insurance exchange for,
        66–67, 74, 83–84
    if you work for, 57–58
    new health care impact on, 1–2
    penalties to, 63
    self-insured, 33
    workplace health coverage, 12
lawsuit, medical, 19, 169–70
legal immigrants, 81–82, 128
Legal Services Corporation, 129
liberals, 88
Lieberman, Joe, 89
lifetime limits, 31–32, 96, 103–4
"limited benefit" health plans, 12–13
    advise on, 13–14
long-term-care insurance, 130–31
loopholes, 5, 14–17, 24
low-income level, time limit for
    uninsured people, 45–46

Maryland, 18–19, 127
Massachusetts Health Connector,
2, 72–73, 82
breast cancer patient costs, 15–16
Georgetown University Health
Policy Institute report, 24
individual mandate, 38–39
maternity, newborn care and, 29, 120
Medicaid, 168–69
agencies, 129
alternatives beyond, 128
benefits, 7, 21, 35, 40, 47, 67, 68
groups covered under new law,
121–22
groups covered under old law,
120–21
health insurance exchanges, 85
new rules effective date, 123
nursing homes, 124
prevalent use of, 119–20
quick changes impacting, 106
subsidies v., 59
what you get through, 124–25
medical devices excise tax, 189–90,
192
medical home, 165–67
Medicare, 3, 7, 8, 21, 35, 37, 46, 68,
168–69
Center for Medicare Advocacy, 118
Congressional Budget Office on,
115
health insurance exchanges, 85
Medicare Advantage plans, 109,
112–15, 181–82, 192
Medicare Rights Center, 117–18
medicare.gov, 117
Medicare.gov Web site, 117
nursing homes, 130–31
payroll tax, 184–85, 192
pilot programs to test, 116
premiums, 183–84, 192
for prescription drugs, 102–3, 106,
108–12, 117, 191
quick changes impacting, 106
subsidies v., 59
Medicare Plus, 87–88
Medicare Rights Center, 117–18, 170

medium-size companies
exchanges open to, 74
with over fifty workers, 44
health insurance exchange for,
66–67, 83–84
if you work for, 57–58
lifetime limits banned, 103–4
new rules impact on, 1–2
penalties to, 63
self-insured companies, 33
workplace health coverage, 12
mental health services, 29
military personnel, 7, 37, 42, 74, 153,
190
minimum benefits package, 28–30
effective date of, 31–32
Minnesota, 18–19
Missouri, 18–19
Multistate Plans, 90–91, 94

National Association of Insurance
Commissioners, 22, 45
National Clearinghouse for
Long-Term Care Information, 140
National Council on Aging, 118
national deficit, 3
program to pay for itself, 52
National Long-Term Care
Ombudsman Resource Center,
140
National Partnership for Women and
Families, 171
Nebraska, "Cornhusker Kickback," 123
Nelson, Ben, 80, 179
"Cornhusker Kickback," 123
Nevada, 40
New Jersey, 18–19
New Mexico, 18–19
new protections, effective dates of,
31–32
New York, 19
newborn care, maternity and, 29
nursing homes, 124, 130–31, 134–40

Obama, Barack, 1, 172
2014, 95
abortion compromise, 80–81

Obama, Barack *(continued)*
  employers fined, 62
  individual mandate, 39–40
  Massachusetts as example, 73
  on prescription filling in Canada,
    112
  program to pay for itself, 52
  on public option, 88–89
Ohio, 19
ombudsman offices, 79, 101–2, 140
"out-of-pocket" expenses, 41
  copayments counting toward,
    15–16
  limits on, 30

Palin, Sarah, 150–51, 154
Partnership for Prevention, 148
Patient Advocate Foundation, 18–19,
    23
Patient-Centered Outcomes Research
    Institute, 152–53
pediatric services, 29, 124, 148, 168
penalties
  for expensive coverage, 63–64
  for not enrolling, 41–42, 63
Pennsylvania, 19, 127
personal care services, 125
Pharmaceutical Research and
    Manufacturers of America,
    111–12
platinum-level plans, 29, 76
Point of Service, 10
poverty line
  expanded coverage, 122
  "free choice voucher," 64
  Medicaid benefits for, 7, 120–22
  premiums v., 40–41
  time limit for uninsured people,
    45–46
  Watson Wyatt Worldwide on, 127
preexisting condition, 4, 8–11, 20, 97
  as of 2014, 17, 26
  effective date/against higher
    premiums, 31–32
  new rules for individual insurance,
    44–45
  time limit for uninsured, 45–46

Preferred Provider Organization, 10
pregnancy, 29, 120
premiums, 2, 4, 20, 43
  advise on shopping for health
    insurance, 13–14
  effective date of protection against
    higher, 31–32
  hikes discouraged, 101
  how subsidies work, 53
  likelihood of cost increase, 27–28
  more spent on health care, 101
  out-of-pocket expenses v., 11–12
  reasons for cost increase, 2, 6, 27
  subsidies v., 40–41
prescription drugs, 29, 125
  advise on shopping for health
    insurance, 14
  copayments for, 11
  Cover Florida Health Care Access
    Program, 12–13
  donut hole in benefits for, 109–12
  effective date/closing "donut hole,"
    110–11
  Medicare, 102–3, 106, 108–12, 117,
    191
preventive and wellness services,
    13, 29, 99, 112, 126, 141–48
Preventive Services Task Force, 112,
    126, 147
private health insurance plans, 7
  kinds of, 10–11
profit motive, 8–9, 25
Project Vote Smart, 59, 86
public option, 87–88
  splitting the difference between
    private and, 90–91

quick changes package
  better appeal rights, 100
  better information on plan options,
    78–79, 99–100
  children's preexisting conditions,
    97
  coverage not canceled for sick
    people, 96–97
  for "donut holes," 102
  effective dates, 102–3

help with costs for early retirees, 100

lifetime limits, 31–32, 96, 103–4

more premiums spent on health care, 101

ombudsman offices, 101–2

premium hikes discouraged, 101

preventive services, 99

small business tax credit, 98–99

stricter rules on annual limits, 96

temporary risk pools, 97–98

young adults on parents' plan, 98, 103–4

rationing, 155–56

rehabilitative services, 29, 125

reinsurance, 20, 69

Republicans, 5. *See also specific person*

campaign to repeal new law, 95

dispute over how to make coverage cheaper, 93–94

on prescription drug coverage, 109

on single-payer system, 88–89

rescissions, 9, 27, 31–32, 45

research

Agency for Healthcare Research and Quality, 147, 152–54

breast cancer costs, 15

can't use, to steer care toward healthier people, 156

Center for Healthcare Decisions, 157

on comparative effectiveness, 152–57, 160

doing your own, 4, 16, 17, 74–75, 104

Employee Benefit Research Institute, 69

Foundation for Informed Medical Decision Making, 171

Henry J. Kaiser Family Foundation, 157

Medicare.gov Web site, 117

on nursing homes, 130–31, 134–36, 139

Patient-Centered Outcomes Research Institute, 152

Pharmaceutical Research and Manufacturers of America, 111

on preventive care, 112, 141–43, 146, 147

resources, 4

community health center, 129

employers required to give information, 65

information on plan options, 78–79, 99–100

Medicaid agencies, 129

retiree, 70. *See also* prescription drugs; seniors

Administration on Aging, 21

early, 35–36, 47, 100, 102, 177

ERISA, 19, 21

health insurance exchanges impacting, 86

National Council on Aging, 118

quick changes impacting, 107

subsidies for, 59–60

temporary "reinsurance" program, 69

Rhode Island, 19

risk pools, 44–45, 97–98

savings account reimbursement, 185–86, 192

Senate Finance Committee, 193

seniors, 7, 35–36, 47, 120. *See also* Medicare; retiree

Administration on Aging, 21

Eldercare Locator, 140

end-of-life care, 140, 150

Federal Administration on Aging, 140

National Clearinghouse for Long-Term Care Information, 140

National Council on Aging, 118

subsidies for, 59–60

SHIPs. *See* State Health Insurance Counseling and Assistance Programs

silver-level plans, 16, 29, 76

small business
    able to join larger pools, 33
    affordable coverage for workers, 8
    health insurance exchange, 2,
        15–16, 66, 74, 83
    if you work for, 56–57
    new rules impact on, 2
    tax credit, 43, 54–56, 98–99, 103
socialism, 5
State Children's Health Insurance
        Program (SCHIP), 7, 35, 38, 42,
        47, 59, 68, 99, 106, 107, 122–24,
        126–27
    health insurance exchanges,
        85–86
state government, 125
    Medicaid paid by, 122–23
    preventive services, 126
    for those outside Medicaid range,
        128
State Health Insurance Counseling
        and Assistance Programs
        (SHIPs), 117, 170
state insurance agencies, 22, 45,
        195–217
    filing complaints with, 18
Stupak, Bart, 80
subsidies, 2, 40–41, 59–60
    applying for, 53–54
    for family of four, 51–52
    how they work, 53
    for individuals, 49–50
substance abuse services, 29
Supplemental Security Income
        program, 120

taxes, 56, 187
    on "Cadillac" Plans, 174–78, 192
    how subsidies work, 53
    Joint Committee on Taxation, 193
    medical devices excise tax, 189–90,
        192
    Medicare payroll tax, 184–85

on retiree drug coverage, 191, 192
    tax credit for small business, 43,
        54–56, 98–99, 103
Tennessee, 19, 68
Texas, 19
TRACER, 7, 74
Treasury Department, 53, 63
TRICARE, 7, 42, 74, 190

underwriting, 20
uninsured
    exemptions, 42–43
    hardship exemptions, 40
    health coverage required v., 37
    health insurance exchanges, 84–85
    if you currently are, 58–59
    income percentage, penalties v., 42
    individual mandate, 37–40
    new protections for, 34–35, 67
    penalties for, 41–42
    quick changes impacting, 105–6
    time limit for, 45–46
United States, profit motive in, 8–9, 25

value-based payments, 162–63
Vermont, 19
Veterans Administration, 7, 37, 42, 74,
        153, 190
Virginia, 18–19
vision care, 29
votesmart.org, 59
voucher, 64–65, 74, 84

wage and price controls, 62
Watson Wyatt Worldwide, 127
Web-based marketplaces, 2
West Virginia, 127
workplace health coverage, 4, 7, 12,
        62, 63–64, 74

X-rays, 124

young adults, 16, 36, 72, 98, 102–4